DEAD FUNNY

Humor in Hitler's Germany

Rudolph Herzog

TRANSLATED BY JEFFERSON CHASE

BROOKLYN, NEW YORK

Dead Funny: Humor in Hitler's Germany
Originally published in German as *Heil Hitler, Das Schwein Ist Tot!*
Lachen unter Hitler—Komik und Humor im Dritten Reich, by Eichborn Verlag
© 2006 by Eichborn AG, Frankfurt am Main, Germany
Translation © 2011 by Jefferson Chase

First Melville House printing: March 2011

Melville House Publishing
145 Plymouth Street
Brooklyn, NY 11201

www.mhpbooks.com

ISBN: 978-1-935554-30-1

Printed in the United States of America

1 2 3 4 5 6 7 8 9 10

Library of Congress Cataloging-in-Publication Data

Herzog, Rudolph.
 [Heil Hitler, das Schwein ist tot! English]
 Dead funny : humor in Hitler's Germany / Rudolph Herzog ; translated by
Jefferson Chase.
     p. cm.
 "Originally published in German as Heil Hitler, das Schwein ist tot! : Lachen
unter Hitler : Komik und Humor im Dritten Reich ... Eichborn Verlag, c2006 ...
Frankfurt am Main, Germany"--T.p. verso.
 Includes bibliographical references and index.
 ISBN 978-1-935554-30-1 (alk. paper)
 1. Germany--Politics and government--1933-1945. 2. National socialism.
3. Holocaust, Jewish, 1939-1945. 4. German wit and humor--History and criticism. 5. Political satire, German--History and criticism. 6. Germany--Politics
and government--1933-1945--Humor. 7. National socialism--Humor. 8. Holocaust, Jewish, 1939-1945--Humor. 9. German wit and humor. 10. Political
satire, German. I. Title.
 DD256.5.H3746913 2011
 943.08602'07--dc22

2011006705

CONTENTS

I. POLITICAL HUMOR UNDER HITLER: AN INSIDE LOOK AT THE THIRD REICH

IS IT PERMISSIBLE to laugh at Hitler? This is a question that is often debated in Germany, where, seeing the magnitude of the horrors the Third Reich committed in their name, many citizens still have difficulty taking a satirical look at it. And when others dare to do precisely that, they are accused of trivializing the Holocaust. Nonetheless, German humorists are always trying to tackle this most sensitive of topics, and jokes at the expense of the Nazis are at their most powerful and revealing when they are spoken in the economical, matter-of-course tone of the satirist.

Is it legitimate to approach Auschwitz using techniques of satire, or would doing so downplay crimes so monstrous that they can hardly be put into words? Whatever one's answer to this question, the fact is that Germans have always laughed at Hitler, even during the twelve years of his terrifying reign. There was no end to political jokes under his regime. Today some of these jokes retain their power, though others seem banal, or simply bad. What they all have in common, however, is the insight they give into what preoccupied and moved Hitler's "racial community." Ordinary people aimed sarcastic remarks at aspects of life that got on their nerves, and Nazi-era humorists—whether they sympathized with the soon to be defunct left-wing opposition or supported the fascist powers-that-were—made political jokes.

By analyzing these jokes, we get unusual access to what people really thought during the "thousand-year Reich," what annoyed them and what made them laugh, and also what they knew and otherwise took pains to repress from their conscious minds. At the same time, the reactions of the Nazi state to challenges from comedians and others who told political jokes reveal what types of humor the fascist leadership actively feared. This book is intended as a journey back to what is thought of as a humorless age, not to make readers laugh but to give them a new perspective on the most terrible era of German history. It does not ignore the moral debates of the postwar period, but it does not focus upon them, either.

The sources used include interviews with people who lived though the Third Reich, among them the friends of a Protestant pastor who was murdered by the Nazis, the son of a famous comedian and animal trainer, and a well-known German cabaret artist. Other important sources were the biographies of prominent German humorists and the various collections of "whispered jokes" that were published in the immediate aftermath of World War II. People who laughed at Hitler within their own four walls, the authors of such compilations tried to suggest, disapproved of the Nazis and were perhaps even part of a tacit resistance. Recent research, however, has revealed that this notion, though a comforting idea, is little more than wishful thinking and historical legend–making.

Political jokes were not a form of resistance. They were a release valve for pent-up popular anger. People told jokes in their neighborhood bars or on the street because they coveted a moment of liberation in which they could let off a bit of steam. That was in the interests of the Nazi leadership, no matter how humorlessly they may have portrayed themselves in the public sphere. Many Germans were conscious of the dark side of the Nazi regime. They were also annoyed at laws forcing them to do this or that and at party bigwigs who treated themselves to lives of luxury while making arbitrary decisions about the lives of others. But that didn't translate into anti-Nazi protests. Those people who let off a bit of steam with a few jokes didn't take to the streets or otherwise challenge the Nazi leadership.

Conversely and significantly, the vast majority of the joke tellers who were denounced and brought before special Nazi courts received a mild punishment, if any. Usually they were let off with a warning. "Whispered jokes" were a surrogate for, and not a manifestation of, social conscience and personal courage. People who lived through the Third Reich also assert that political jokes were by no means spoken only in hushed tones in the private sphere. Only during the final phase of the war, when it was clear Germany was losing, were draconian punishments handed down for people who made fun of the Nazis. They will be discussed later in this book. As the Nazi system entered its death throes and tried to resist its inevitable demise, there were a conspicuous number of especially cutting jokes, but we have no way of knowing precisely how widespread they were.

The vast majority of political jokes during Hitler's reign were basically uncritical of the system, playing on the human weaknesses of Nazi leaders rather than on the crimes they were committing. Imperial Marshal Hermann Göring, for instance, was a popular target because of his pompous appearance and his love of glamour and medals. One typical joke ran:

> *Göring recently added an arrow to the many medals on his chest. It's there as a directional sign: "To be continued on my back."*

Like many Göring jokes, the tone here is familial and affectionate, rather than harsh. The political humor of the time never alluded to the fact that Göring was a sadist who became a mass murderer as well. On the contrary, the imperial marshal appears most often as a sort of pompous but ultimately likeable Falstaff. In fact, Göring's all too apparent human weaknesses endeared the second most powerful man in the Third Reich to broad segments of the population. The fact that he was a cold-blooded, cynical despot with no regard for human dignity did not prevent Germans from sympathizing with him right up to his postwar suicide while in Allied captivity.

THERE WERE SOME JOKES, of course, that expressed sheer hatred for and rejection of the Nazi regime. These were known in Berlin, with its coarse, blunt, cosmopolitan sense of humor, as surefire jokes not because they were certain to get a laugh but because they were guaranteed to land anyone caught telling them in front of a firing squad or the middle of a concentration camp. But a good argument could be made that even these most critical jokes ultimately served to stabilize the system. For though some jokes expressed dissatisfaction with the Nazi regime, they also conveyed the message that there was nothing anyone could do about it—a message of paralyzing fatalism. For example, one joke during the Third Reich parodied the Nazi slogan "The Führer leads and we follow" as "The Führer takes the lead and we take what follows." The subtext was that ordinary Germans had no means of affecting disastrous decisions made from on high. Another joke, which was popular in Vienna after Germany's annexation of Austria, was similar in tone:

A poster for the Winter Relief Fund reads: "No one should

*be allowed to go hungry or suffer from the cold." A work-
ersays to a colleague: "So now we're not even allowed to do
that."*

The Winter Relief Fund was a propagandistically inspired Nazi
charity that helped poorer Germans with heating and other costs
in the colder months of the year.

The resigned attitude expressed in such humor was not
unique to jokes told by Germans with what the Nazis considered the proper racial pedigree. It was typical of Jewish humor
too, where it had a harder edge and much sharper sarcasm. One
typical Jewish joke plays on the color of the fascists' trademark
uniforms:

*A Swiss visiting a Jewish friend in the Third Reich asks him:
"So how do you feel under the Nazis?" He answers: "Like a
tapeworm. Every day, I wriggle my way through a mass of
brown stuff and wait to be excreted."*

But the fundamental difference between German and German-
Jewish jokes was less a matter of tone or edge than of function.
Whereas "whispered jokes" among Germans served primarily as
a release valve for pent-up popular frustration, jokes told by their
Jewish countrymen can be interpreted as an attempt to muster
courage—or, as the great compiler of Jewish-German jokes Salcia
Landmann put it, as an expression of Jews' will to survive against
all odds. These jokes make fun of the terrors Jews experienced
every day. As such, the blackest Jewish humor expresses defiance:
I laugh, therefore I am. My back is to the wall, and I'm still laughing. One example from the final years of World War II takes this
attitude to a macabre extreme:

Two Jews are waiting to face a firing squad, when the news arrives that they are to be hanged instead. One turns to the other and says: "You see—they've run out of ammunition!"

The situation for these two Jews may be hopeless, says the punch line, but there's hope for the Jewish people: the Nazi regime is about to collapse.

Jewish humor was uniquely bleak and pulled no punches. The contrast in message and tone between this joke and the toothless gag about Göring's medals could hardly be more stark. It demonstrates with painful clarity how drastically the perspective of Hitler's victims diverged from that of the millions of accessories to the Führer's crimes.

HUMOR IS NOT just determined by the group affiliations of its makers and audience. It can only be understood with reference to the social context of its time. Many of the jokes in this book, especially those of the professional humorists and comedians of the Nazi era, can barely be recognized as funny today. It's difficult for us to imagine that people could have laughed at jests so stale, superficial, and sedate. What makes them important today is the way they reflect, as all old jokes do, what truly occupied, amused, and annoyed the people of their time. They open a window on the Third Reich, giving us an inside view more authentic in its way than can be found in official historical documents.

Modern Germans don't like to admit it, but their perception of the Hitler years is based largely on the propaganda films of the era. Weekly newsreels and Leni Riefenstahl's films are the artifacts their documentaries always cite—artifacts that were calculated and ideologically tainted. They were never a representation of reality or an expression of what was truly going on in the Nazi system. Even today they deceive the viewer, through the force of images that even the most cautionary commentary can hardly put into proper context.

But our distorted perspective cannot be blamed solely on cinematic documents of the Nazi era. Our historic hindsight also plays a role. We observe the Third Reich in retrospect, knowing all too well where the path taken by this evil system will end. The horrors of the Holocaust and Hitler's wars of annihilation are so present in today's collective consciousness that the years leading up to those crimes against humanity have been pushed into the background. So we lose sight of thousands of instances where the screws were gradually tightened to choke off the rule of law and then almost any form of humane behavior. At the beginning of their regime, the Nazi's hold on power was anything but unbreakable. The earliest phase of Nazi rule was dominated by *Gleichschaltung*, which meant, roughly, "getting Germans into the same ideological gear," a policy that the National Socialists carried out by silencing or murdering the majority of their critics. But even this brutality could not reform German society as it had been during the Weimar Republic into a racially based, Nazi folk community overnight. Jokes from the early years of Nazi rule, including those of professional comedians, give us particular insight into the mood of the populace. These jokes comment upon and make fun of the political events of the day and throw a harshly revealing light on certain social transformations, though other social processes that may appear more significant from today's perspective are hardly mentioned.

As members of the Nazi secret police wrote in their reports, the people generally stood behind Hitler in the years before World War II, despite the hard line that those in power were taking. The bubbling enthusiasm depicted in weekly German newsreels may have been an exaggeration, but the majority of Germans were satisfied with their government, which seemed to have had an especially lucky hand in the realm of foreign relations. This satisfaction was reflected in contemporary political jokes, which were largely harmless and silly. Only with the onset of World War II did the citizens' mood begin to shift significantly. And with Germany's military defeat at Stalingrad and the first waves of Allied bombing campaigns against German cities, German political humor took on a dark, fatalist tone. Silliness gave way to sarcasm.

By describing how and why people laughed during the Third Reich, this book aims to examine the sensibilities of the German people—and all of the changes to which those sensibilities were subject—during the twelve years of Nazi dictatorship. What this clarifies among other things is that the Third Reich was not nearly as monolithic as the makers of contemporary newsreels liked to depict it. Nazi society remained heterogeneous, influenced by very diverse interests, frustrations, worries, and fears, all of which were reflected in the humor of the time.

II. THE RISE AND DEVELOPMENT OF POLITICAL HUMOR

MOST POLITICAL JOKES can be seen as attacks, launched by humorous means, on those in power or on prevailing political conditions. Through comic exaggeration they make the state and its representatives seem laughable. Many of these jokes are told in a winking spirit of fun; in others, there is an underlying bitterness. But even the tellers of this second kind of political joke are not necessarily rebelling against the system. Political humor is not, in and of itself, a form of resistance; on the contrary, political humorists, like the dog in the old adage, usually have a bark that's worse than their bite.

Political humor is often described as a relatively recent historical phenomenon. In older epochs, so the argument runs, the power of the state was not legitimized by the people, but by God, so any criticism of those in power was blasphemy and therefore punishable by church condemnation and state law. Thus, political jokes could only arise in the modern, secular world. This theory is sound up to a point: it is true that the political humor was able to develop as a genre only in modern times. The reason for that, however, was not so much that the Western world became more secular but rather that relations of power became more complicated. After the French Revolution, the ways in which the people and their representatives interacted were far more multifaceted than before. The number of targets available for satirical attack increased as opportunities for citizens to express criticism broadened. This does not mean that there can be no political humor in states that are legitimized by the prevailing concept of the divine. Modern theocracies such as the current Iranian state, as well as ancient Rome, prove the contrary. Those who maintain otherwise deny the essential human quality of political humor, the impulse to dispute the ideal image that all systems claiming divine legitimacy try to project. People enjoy laughing at their leaders. That has always been the case and will continue to be so. It makes no difference whether such laughter is legal or not, or whether it is considered an insult to His Majesty or an offense against God.

Images from ancient Rome leave no doubt that Romans aggressively went after the weaknesses of their leaders. Busts of those in power are uncompromisingly realistic. Emperors are depicted with Adam's apples protruding like birds' craws; senators sport double chins. Unlike the ancient Greeks, the Romans were positively obsessed with human defects, and that is also reflected in their choice of names. Was Barabbas called that because he had a big bushy beard? The Romans gleefully handed out sobriquets based on a person's limp, baldness, or harelip—using seemingly unlimited imagination to tag their victims.

Romans were equally creative with insults of every kind, and their love of the obscene is well known. Politicians constantly insulted one another, and the people enjoyed passing these barbs on as racy gossip. Most of those in power calmly put up with such indignities, as the following anecdote, which had no consequences for the man who told it, attests:

> Somewhere in the Empire a man was found who bore a striking resemblance to Augustus Caesar. He was introduced to the emperor, who, surprised at the existence of

*this doppelgänger, asked him, "Tell me, was your mother
ever in Rome?" "No," answered the man, "but my father
sure was."*

Political barbs hit the mark, then as now, wherever an Achilles'
heel was to be found and aimed at, and the higher the pedestal on
which the heel rested, the better. Emperors, dictators and other
big shots who rule on the basis of sublime principles have a long
distance to fall. Thus they quickly became favorite targets for biting scorn.

Rulers who would represent the ideal, of course, are measured
by their own ambition and conceit. If too great a discrepancy is
perceived between the ideal and reality, if a ruler has clearly set
the bar too high, he opens himself up to humorous attack. So
a godlike emperor became a fop of dubious parentage, and the
member of a popular tribunal became a senile old man with a
crooked nose. This sort of ridicule can be found not just in modern history, but in antiquity and the Middle Ages as well.

IT IS TELLING that a compilation of "whispered jokes" was
one of the first books to be published in postwar Germany. That
fact reflects not just Germans' eagerness to exonerate themselves,
since such jokes were taken as a sign of "resistance" against Hitler, but also a basic human need. It was neither astonishing nor
new that people should try to use laughter to deal with traumatic
events. There are many comparable examples in both the rest of
German and world history, and one doesn't have to search far to
find them.

Readers encounter an example of this phenomenon in early
modern times, in the wake of the Thirty Years' War. Europe lay in

ruins, and whole stretches of territory had been depopulated. In Southern Germany, one of the most heavily devastated regions, barely a third of the population had survived. Many who had not died in battle fell victim to starvation and disease. In the initial years after this unprecedented hurricane of destruction, little was said or done to condemn it. Then suddenly, in 1699, Hans Jakob Christoffel von Grimmelshausen raised his voice, in the first adventure novel ever published in German. The absurd pseudonym the author used, Scheifheim von Sulsfort, was a preview of what readers would find inside the novel's pages. *The Adventures of Simplicius Simplicissimus*, the first major literary work after the apocalypse of the Thirty Years' War, was a book full of jokes.

The novel's hero, a simple shepherd, stumbles through the war in a variety of roles, from a doctoring quack to a cowskin-dressed fool. The wholesale arson, murder, and rape going on around him serve as the backdrop for his roguish pranks. Readers see a bizarrely distorted reality through the eyes of the protagonist-fool, who was raised like a wild animal. As a young boy, Simplicissimus endured terrible suffering, but his descriptions of the horrors that he himself went through are cheerful and disarmingly ironic. Even when a splinter group of soldiers attacks his boyhood home and murders his stepparents, the narrative remains grotesquely nonchalant:

The first thing these knights did was to tie up their horses, whereupon each one went about his strange tasks, all of which yielded demise and ruin. While some of them set about to butcher, boil, and roast, others stormed the house from top to bottom. Even the secret master chamber was not safe, as if the Golden Fleece were concealed within.

Grimmelshausen himself took part in the Thirty Years' War, and the novel is full of autobiographical detail. The author takes the terrible slaughter he had survived and turns it into farce.

At first glance a novel featuring a rogue hero but really about a decades-long bloodbath may itself seem like a bizarre idea. Why didn't Grimmelshausen just write a chronicle of events? The message of *Simplicissimus* is that fear and terror are only half as bad when one can laugh in their face.

Ironically, the tradition of the German novel begins with the sort of humor that still occasions controversy today, when people try to treat Hitler comically. Yet the truth is that terrible events seem to call for humor. In the aftermath of a catastrophe, humor often appears as the only effective antidote against lingering horror. One could cite dozens of examples of how the deepest human abysses make people laugh. The mentality underlying Grimmelshausen's black humor is also found in Jewish humor.

JUST AS THE LESS THAN IDEAL Roman emperors inspired ridicule, the leaders of the Nazi empire were constantly being compared with the Aryan models they promoted. "Dear God, please make me blind so that I can tell myself Goebbels looks Aryan," was a popular quip at the time. Whether or not this "prayer" is a verbal attack or a harmless joke is beside the point. It is more notable that, whatever way you take it, this type of German political humor blossomed under totalitarian rule, rather than in an open, free, and democratic society. Countless cabaret artists may make fun of present-day German politicians, but, just as in the Weimar Republic, spontaneously invented, popular political jokes are not nearly as common today as they were in the Third Reich or Communist East Germany.

Examined in retrospect, Wilhelmine Germany appears to fall in between these two extremes. Few political jokes from that time have been recorded, but this may have more to do with researchers' lack of interest than with the period's lack of antigovernment satire. The scholar Ralph Wiener has compiled a few examples. They consist of benign *bon mots* and short anecdotes as ornately baroque as the monarchy for which they were invented. Political humor under the kaiser only turned truly absurd and biting when its target was the ominous growth of militarism. The unthinking obedience of Prussian soldiers and the explosion of the imperial bureaucracy were easy marks for jesters in Wilhelm's Germany.

The following example is one of the better jokes of the time:

> *During a native rebellion in German East Africa, the Imperial Ministry in Berlin issued the following order to its representatives on the ground: "The natives are to be instructed that on pain of harsh penalties, every rebellion must be announced, in writing, six weeks before it breaks out."*

The joke isn't all that funny from our perspective, but it does feature a number of phenomena typical of the age, including the misguided and brutal behavior of the belatedly colonial German power and the impossibly wordy bureaucratic language of imperial government employees, which not even their African subjects were spared. For citizens of the Wilhelmine Empire, the punch line may have had a crude charm—an appeal we can only imagine today.

The imperial leadership was pigheaded and complacent, and the rules governing who was on top and who was subordinate were firmly fixed. The bureaucracy was outmoded and prone to intervening in people's lives. In general, Wilhelmine Germans made their peace with the antiquated social order. From lofty heights, the German kaiser steered the state, which often seemed to be amazed and somewhat afraid of how big it had become. Kaiser Wilhelm II, with his waxed moustache, had little to do with mere mortals, appearing to many more like a monument to himself than a man made of flesh and blood.

But the posturing of the German leadership was by no means lost on the people, and jokes from this period often poked fun at the kaiser's otherwordliness and vanity. But these humorous remarks at Wilhelm II's expense were relatively bloodless and innocuous. Even the following joke, aimed at the cult of personality surrounding the monarch, lacks any real force from today's standards:

> *A customer goes into the gifts section of a big department store to buy himself a keepsake. But all he sees are busts and more busts of the Kaiser. They're made of plaster, and there's no visible difference between any of them. The customer stands there at a loss, until a salesman walks up, coughs, and asks politely: "Have you made your selection?"*

There's little tension at work here. The punch line is completely soft—no amount of imagination can read anything comical, biting, or critical into it. The joke points up the absurdity of the omnipresence of a kaiser who's already become a monument, but it clearly isn't intended to do anything more than make listeners smile a bit.

Likewise harmless, although somewhat more bold, was the first publication by Kurt Tucholsky, the Berlin native who became Weimar Germany's greatest satirist. In 1907, he was held back in school due to poor marks in German composition. But on November 22 of that year, the 17-year-old had a short piece entitled "Fairy Tale" in the satirical magazine *Ulk*:

There once was a Kaiser who ruled over an endlessly big, rich and beautiful land. Like all other emperors, he possessed a chamber full of treasures in which, amidst all of the shining and glittering jewels, there was a piper's pipe. It was a strange instrument. When one looked through one of its four holes, what wonders there were to see! There was a landscape, tiny but full of life: a Thomas landscape with clouds by Böcklin and lakes by Leistikov. Tiny women in the style of Reznicek turned up their noses at figures by the caricaturist Zille, and a Meunier farm girl carried an armful of flowers by Orlik. In short, the whole of "modern" German art was in the pipe. And the Kaiser? He couldn't give a whistle.

Tucholsky's text takes the monarch's mundane taste in art to task. Wilhelm II was interested in neither in the miniature figures of Constantin Meunier nor still-lifes by the poet Rilke's associate Emil Orlik. Everything new and modern that fascinated the 17-year-old Tucholsky simply bounced off the emperor, who was stuck in the past. The ruler in this fairy tale can't see the trees for the forest. He has no idea what great talents his empire contains.

On the other hand, the fact that the Germans' brittle, inflexible ruler would lead them into a world war, whose dimensions he himself anticipated less clearly than anyone, never became a topic for political jokes. Germans' enthusiasm for the war and their effusive patriotism were initially too naïve, and the disappointment that followed came too abruptly. Wilhelm II was unable to deliver the proverbial stroll through Paris. Instead, what the German populace got was a torturously long and extremely brutal war of hardened fronts, which ended in the German Empire's defeat. Yet it was only after the end that German satirists discovered the war as a topic. Among these writers was Kurt Tucholsky, whose journalistic career had been interrupted when he was called to serve at the front.

HIS DEFEAT drove the kaiser out of Germany, but the pomposity, obsession with military discipline, and other negative artifacts of Prussian culture remained. After Wilhelm II fled, in 1918, conservatives began to consider Paul von Hindenburg, and in 1925 the field marshal was elected imperial president—a kind of ersatz kaiser. This strange figure never really fit into Weimar's democracy and modernized state. His thinking, behavior, and entire appearance were too oriented toward the past. It's not surprising that Germans particularly enjoyed laughing at and cracking jokes about this relic of a lost epoch.

Yet again, the jokes were tame and innocuous, even affectionate. The following example of wit is a declaration of love in disguise:

After the Battle of Tannenberg in 1914, Field Marshal Paul von Hindenburg visited Frankfurt am Main. He stopped in front of a building he didn't know and asked what it was. "That's St. Paul's Cathedral," someone explained. With characteristic modesty, Hindenburg replied: "Oh, you shouldn't have bothered, I'm just here for a few days."

The joke plays upon Hindenburg's outsize ego and also,

incidentally, upon his presumed ignorance of democratic history: St. Paul's Cathedral was where the first German national assembly convened in the revolutionary year of 1848. But his cluelessness, like his conceit, is depicted sympathetically, as a forgivable, human flaw.

The same basic joke was told in the Third Reich about Hermann Göring: Imperial Marshal Göring visits the monument to the Germanic tribal leader Hermann in the Teutoburger Forest and says, "Oh, you shouldn't have." A great many Hindenburg jokes were to reappear a decade later as Göring quips. The reason was simple. Both men had a love of pompous public appearances and Byzantine splendor, and both men's chests were covered with medals. One popular Hindenburg joke likely predated the Weimar Republic:

Saint Peter's complaint: "Every time Hindenburg visits for the weekend, I find a star missing."

This gentle joke was also told on Göring during the Third Reich. And, just as when it was aimed at Hindenburg, it carried no real sting. On the contrary, it was a verbal congé before its subject, no criticism, but rather an expression of admiration and respect for that many-medaled chest, despite or perhaps precisely because of the decorated man's childish love of publicly displaying his honors. Indeed, there is no detectable hatred for party bigwigs in jokes like this from the Third Reich, despite what many editors who compiled such "whispered jokes" after the end of Nazism tried to suggest.

Neither of the jokes cited above is spontaneous or sarcastic, and the basic anecdote presumably existed in some form long before either. They belong to that genre of political humor in which the shell of an ancient jest is simply refilled with content appropriate to its time. Some patterns of human behavior are so obvious, they can survive any change of system or regime. At heart, such jokes are apolitical, even when they are aimed at a well-known political figure. The following joke has enjoyed a special longevity:

> *In Germany, a new measure is to be introduced. One Gör equals the maximum number of medals that can be hung on a single human chest.*

In Communist East Germany, the name of the measure was changed to redirect the punch line at party secretary and political leader Walther Ulbricht and a famously sycophantic news presenter on East German TV, Eduard von Schnitzler:

> *In East Germany, a new measure was introduced at the end of the Sixties: the Ulb.*
> *One Ulb was the time an East German needed to get out of his chair and change the channel when the secretary was speaking on TV. And what was one one-hundredth of an Ulb? A Schnitz.*

Thus, the joke was not only adapted to postwar Communist society but also expanded for it. The idea of the punch line isn't augmented, however; it is merely repeated, making the joke wordier and significantly reducing its comic effectiveness.

The joke still worked in Communist East Germany thanks not to its topicality but to its formula, which raises curiosity, builds tension, and then ends with a clever punch line. Both the Nazi and the Communist variations can be classified as political only because their subjects are members of the ruling class. These leaders are being called vain and soporific, but neither foible is a grotesque violation of social norms or an atrocity against civilization, so the jokes don't carry much subversive political force. They are pleasant tricks of language intended to raise a smile, nothing more and nothing less.

The following riddle, which appeared toward the end of World War I, is somewhat more critical:

Who would be saved if the Kaiser, the Chancellor, and their generals all capsized while on a voyage at sea? Germany.

The same joke was told at the end of World War II, with Hitler, Göring, and Goebbels as the men overboard. For 17 years, this subversive riddle had been forgotten, then retrieved from the mothballs as German cities were being bombarded and the Nazi reign of terror was in its death throes. But although the joke expresses the hope that the political leadership will be destroyed, it is more fatalistic than incendiary. The country is saved by a fortuitous accident, by the superhuman power of the sea—not by a human revolt. The German people are not called to rebellion but told to pray for rescue through an unlikely twist of fate. In another variation of the joke, Hitler is sitting in a bunker and gets hit by a bomb. In that case, the enemy—still not the German people—takes over nature's role as tyrannicide.

A third formulaic joke, which had an even longer history, lacked the bitter sarcasm of the previous example—in its original form. It was first told at the expense of Gustav Stresemann, a chancellor and later a foreign minister during the Weimar Republic who was constantly under attack for signing controversial international agreements:

Stresemann is traveling by train, and the engineer has to stop at a small station because of damage to the tracks ahead. The station master is then arrested. Why? Because just as Stresemann is alighting, the unfortunate employee says to the panicky passengers, "Please step down."

The punch line, a call for Stresemann to resign, is a bit of needling and would not have gotten the teller in much trouble in a democratic system. But in the context of a dictatorship, such a joke becomes considerably more explosive. According to a report by a contemporary, Carl Schulz, the Berlin cabaret artist Werner Finck performed a Hitler sketch along lines similar to this joke just before the start of World War II. It took courage to mount the stage before the eyes of the secret police and informants who might have been in the audience. Schulz describes the scene:

After the Nazis came to power, a decree was issued that a picture of Hitler must be hung in all government offices. Werner Finck created a comic routine out of it... Willi Schaeffer [the director of the cabaret] carried a picture onto the stage so that the audience could only see the back. Everyone in the audience, though, thought, "That's a picture of Hitler." Suddenly Schaeffer stumbled and almost dropped it. Finck hurried up to him, calling out, "Don't topple, don't topple!"—which was greeted with uproarious laughter.

Today, the punch line of this routine may seem weak, but considering the tense mood in Nazi Germany before the beginning of World War II, the sketch was not without subversive force. No one was permitted to think out loud in public about Hitler being toppled. Finck's cheeky sketch lived from what *wasn't* seen but *did* take place in the mind of the audience. The fact that people laughed showed they got the joke.

When people made fun of their aged imperial president in the final years of the Weimar Republic, there was no need for subterfuge. The unpopular democracy was on its last legs, as was the state's highest representative. In the years leading up to his death, Paul von Hindenburg had increasingly withdrawn from public life. He lived in isolation on his estate, surrounded by people he patronized and by sycophants. The Prussian field marshal had delegated most of his authority to the government cabinet, which happily went on with business as usual while a great political catastrophe loomed.

The checks and balances written into Weimar's political system proved entirely inadequate to control the Führer of the Nazi Party. Hindenburg's proxies—his own son, Oskar, and his deputy, Otto Meissner, were no match for Hitler, who had worked his way up from Bavarian local politics all the way to Berlin. Hindenburg himself was the only national politician who could have restrained the provincial demagogue. But the aging leader was as uninterested as the electorate in preserving the unpopular Weimar state. However, the Germans were not so disaffected from politics as not to register their president's gradual loss of power. They did, and made it the backdrop of the following joke, popular in Berlin:

> *One day, Oskar von Hindenburg and Otto Meissner were quarreling about who should make a decision in their leader's name. In the end, Meissner said, "Listen, who's president here? You or me?"*

It was not lost on many Germans that neither Oskar von Hindenburg nor Meissner would be able to fill the old patriarch's shoes. At the same time, rumors and jokes arose about the patriarch's alleged increasing senility.

According to one story, after Hitler came to meet Hindenburg at his estate, Gut Neudeck, the president asked since when had Heinrich Brüning (a former German chancellor) worn a moustache. The anecdote was likely apocryphal, but it presaged in an uncanny way what was to happen in reality—at least, according to Hitler himself, who claimed that at his last meeting with the deathly ill field marshal, Hindenburg had addressed him as "Your Majesty."

Another joke that made the rounds in a number of variations in the late Weimar Republic is difficult to translate because it plays on the dual meaning of the German word *Blatt*, "leaf" and "sheet of paper":

> *A street cleaner is seen raking up leaves in front of the presidential palace for the tenth time in one day. A passerby asks him, "Why are you sweeping up again?" He answers, "Because otherwise, the president will sign them."*

The point—that the president would sign anything—was prophetic. The Weimar Republic essentially ended with Hindenburg's signature on a piece of paper making Adolf Hitler chancellor of Germany.

A LOT HAS been written about the last days of the dying democracy and the Nazis' rise to power, and there's no need to repeat it here. The Nazi dictatorship meant the disappearance of the society which had produced the flourishing cultural life of the "Golden Twenties," a paradise for those who had the opportunity and financial resources to take part in it.

For satirists and comedians, the Weimar era was a time of relative prosperity. Especially in the glitzy metropolis of Berlin, cabaret stages and cellar theaters sprouted up everywhere, and the German film company UFA made countless comedies directly outside the gates of the city. The studio's director was the unlikeable and arrogant Alfred Hugenbuerg, a man of extreme right-wing sensibilities who created silly comedies to distract the populace, plagued by inflation and unemployment, from their grim everyday lives. Most of these apolitical productions have been forgotten—and rightly so. One exception was the huge 1930 hit *The Three From the Gas Station*, starring the comic actor Heinz Rühmann. It is still watched today. The persistent popularity of this naively funny film can scarcely be explained by its simple story line. The secret to its rather childish charm was its cleverly paced musical interludes. Songs like "A friend, a friend, there's nothing better in the world..." are still well known in Germany.

The complicated and often utterly silly gags, which took up more space in the film than the plot, are easily forgivable as products of the age. The film doesn't pile on action at the hectic tempo of the postmodern era. Instead, it draws its life from the affirmative allure of the Golden Twenties.

A cast of stars also ensured the film's mass appeal. *The Three from the Gas Station* marked the beginning of the mercurial rise of the young comedian Rühmann, who quickly became a national star and a personal favorite of Goebbels, while a far less happy fate befell his costar, the Jewish cabaret performer Kurt Gerron. In *The Three from the Gas Station*, Gerron portrays a brash lawyer who informs the film's hero, in a singularly absurd fashion, that they're bankrupt. One of the high points of the picture was an almost dadaistic telephone exchange between Rühmann and Gerron. It was the collision of two talents, a young one with a bright future and an older one who was already beyond the zenith of his career.

Gerron, who had excelled in the role of the dubious magician in Josef von Sternberg's *The Blue Angel*, enjoyed a successful directorial career in the early 1930s. But he was best remembered as a likeable overweight character actor. His and his fellow Jewish comedians set the tone for the years between the wars. The humorous world of the Twenties was fast-paced, full of cabaret performers, clowns, and satirists such as Gerron or Otto Wallburg, who in some fifty films played a wide range of well-meaning characters, from average Joes up to state consuls. Above all, Wallburg was popular for his strange, stuttering speech, or "blubbering," which attracted no shortage of imitators. Another important figure was Willy Rosen, whose smart musical arrangements delighted audiences in a number of prominent Berlin theaters, including the Scala and Kabarett der Komiker.

In Vienna, which was the other capital of Jewish humor, second only to Berlin, there was the brilliant Fritz Grünbaum, a small, weaselly, sharp-tongued actor, and his partner, Karl Farkas, a man with a large crooked nose and an amazing talent for improvisation. Farkas was known for his ability to spontaneously come up with rhymes for words called out by the audience. A contemporary wrote of his act:

Once an anti-Semite in the audience tried to provoke him, challenging him to find a rhyme for "Jewish thief." He took a rose from a vase and said: "Here is the rose, and there is the leaf. Here is the Jew, and there is the thief."

Grünbaum and Farkas were the Viennese equivalent of Laurel and Hardy in terms of both fame and popularity. Paul Morgan was another popular comic actor; Friedrich Hollaender composed much of the music used in the acts. The list could go on. It was a golden age of Jewish comedy, and all of Austria laughed along with the stars. But within a few years, all that was over. The witty remarks about everyday life, the ironic couplets and the clever dialogues fell silent. Some Jewish comedians went into exile. But Kurt Gerron, Otto Wallburg, Willy Rosen, Fritz Grünbaum, along with many others, died in Hitler's death camps.

III. THE NAZI SEIZURE OF POWER

WHEN THE NAZIS came to power in 1933, they had already passed the zenith of their popularity. In the national elections of November 6, 1932, the NSDAP, or (National Socialist German Workers' Party) had remained the strongest party, but it had lost roughly two million votes and 34 seats in parliament, mostly to parties on the far left and the conservative nationalists. The path to power seemed blocked, but weaknesses within the political system of the Weimar Republic conspired with the unhappy constellation of leaders at the head of the German state to allow Hitler to become chancellor the following year. In retrospect, it is all too obvious that mainstream politicians underestimated the Nazi leader, who easily played off his nondescript rivals against one another.

Still, it's difficult to comprehend how the political establishment could have allowed itself to be so manipulated. In public appearances Hitler vacillated between awkwardness and arrogance and often came off as little more than a beer tent–inspired blowhard. Nazi party events were as shrill as they were seductive, and their leader cut a bizarre figure, conflating Jews and "Bolsheviks" in endless tirades and preaching the values of Germanness while publishing garbled books written in miserable German. The pillars of Weimar society would have known all too well how deluded and extremist Nazi ideology was, and perhaps for that reason they failed to understand how dangerous its chief exponent could be. On the contrary, they thought they could tame the upstart Hitler by giving him political responsibility. Few of his contemporaries realized that he was not just a flash-in-the-pan demagogue but instead a cunning tactician who knew how to maneuver and modulate his positions.

Most bourgeois Germans associated the NSDAP with the thugs of the SA stormtroopers, the Sturmabteilung, who marched through the streets in baggy military pants making a lot of noise. Their self-appointed "Führer" with his ridiculous moustache was criminally underrated. For instance, the author of this police report from 1927 was singularly unimpressed by Hitler's oratory:

> [Hitler] speaks without notes, initially in drawn-out fashion for emphasis. Later on, the words come tumbling out, and in overly dramatic passages, his voice is strained and barely understandable. He waves his hands and arms around, jumps back and forth excitably, and always seems to be trying to captivate his attentive, thousand-strong audience. When he's interrupted by applause, he theatrically stretches out his hands. The word *no*, which occurs repeatedly toward the end of his speech, is stagy and pointedly emphasized. In and of itself, his talent as a speaker was ... for this reporter nothing special.

Hitler as a comic figure? When bizarre ranks of brown-shirted SA men marched past, singing "Germanic" songs, many left-wing intellectual observers at the time didn't know whether they should laugh or cry.

The new political movement was both pompous and grotesque, and Hitler's appointment as German chancellor probably seemed to his many German detractors like a bad joke. One contemporary recalls the Nazis' triumphant marches after Hitler attained power:

In the torchlight, the faces under their SA caps almost resembled those of the martial warriors from the Nazis' propaganda posters. We had often mocked those Nordic profiles. We knew the dull visages of our adversaries all too well. But now here they were, actually marching past us, intoxicated by their triumph, bellowing out their idiotic favorite song: "When Jewish blood squirts from the knife, happy days will return."

But these troops of thugs and their leadership were serious about their murderous words. "Now, the cleansing process will commence in all areas," Hitler's chief ideologue, Alfred Rosenberg, declared shortly after the party seized power.

In January 1933, Hitler's cabinet met for the first time, with the Nazi leader ostensibly under the restraining influence of his coalition partners from the mainstream parties. But the representatives of political reason soon fell under the sway of Hitler's lupine charm. Like the audience in the street, they were blinded by the marches and propagandistic spectacles in the initial days of the Nazi-led government and quickly became little more than marionettes, as Hitler moved to consolidate his authority. The spirit of the times, so it seemed, favored the National Socialists. With breathtaking rapidity, Hitler carried out his plans for getting rid of multiparty democracy by "legal" means. He was able to do so not just because the Nazis acted ruthlessly and effectively, but because competing political forces put up a halfhearted resistance. The general mood among the citizenry also undermined the ability of the Weimar state to resist the attack from within. Hitler succeeded in channeling the emotional energies released by the Nazi ascent to power into a feeling that things were getting better. The new enthusiasm engendered in the political mainstream was accompanied by a sense of relief, even joy, that democracy was coming to an end. Many Germans felt that the system was ineffective, outmoded, and incapable of solving problems. Hitler achieved overnight what the Weimar Republic had been unable to do in fifteen years: he won over the hearts of the people.

With this change in the political mood and the growing desire for a strong political leadership, criticism of Hitler receded into the background. German humor, too, changed sides. Many comedians aligned themselves with the political winners, although that didn't make their jokes any funnier. Cabaret performer Dieter Hildebrandt, who spent his boyhood in the Third Reich, recalls an evening of entertainment staged by the Hitler Youth, in which the older members played a cabaret skit skewering Weimar politics:

> "What moved people in Germany, what made them split their sides laughing, was the musty old Weimar Republic and its democracy. The entire public shared this view, and they rolled on the floor giggling. On the evening in question, the skit was set in parliament. One of the boys, dressed as a parliamentary deputy, slept the entire time. When suddenly an alarm clock went off, the audience cried with delight. Another deputy had a speech impediment; a third, a problem with flatulence. The entire evening was devoted to making fun of a democracy that had passed its sell-by date, and the audience couldn't get enough. That was the mood. Even back then, there was a saying: Germans didn't just reject democracy—they positively hated it. But they didn't want their former monarchy back, either. That also put them off. In this sense, the Nazis arrived on the scene at precisely the right moment."

The only aspect of the Nazis' rise that attracted popular displeasure was the abruptness with which party bigwigs seized coveted positions in society. On every front, from the police force to civic offices, people were pushed out of their jobs and replaced ↵ by party loyalists. The speed with which this happened was unprecedented. For example, in Germany's largest bureaucracy, the Prussian Interior Ministry, dozens of "voluntary commissioners" were appointed for the purposes of political "cleansing." They immediately began firing people and hiring replacements.

Not everyone was pleased by the new career paths opening up for fascist loyalists, and the jokes of the period include a number of barbs directed at Nazi social climbers. More than anything, people were concerned about their own welfare, which suddenly seemed in doubt. What happens if your new director, superior commissioner, or department head is a Nazi? How do you reach an arrangement with the new fascist bosses? These were the worries expressed in a number of sarcastic jokes. One untranslatable example played on the party acronym, NSDAP. The letters, as the joke ran, actually stood for "Na? Suchst du auch Pöstchen?"— "So, you're looking for a comfy little job as well?" For non-party members, the fear of losing positions of authority and privilege to Nazis was hardly unreasonable, and such worries stirred Germans far more than any concern for their Jewish fellow citizens or for members of the political opposition, even though the Nazis left no doubt that the future would be most unpleasant for both groups. Charity, as far as the future was concerned, began at home.

Interviewing witnesses to this history and analyzing jokes from the time about fascist officeholders and unofficial community sheriffs, one quickly comes to the conclusion that the citizens of Hitler's Germany did not take small-time Nazis very seriously at this point. Germans did not see them as the executors of a deeply

criminal regime but rather as brazenly comic figures who were el-
bowing their way into the public sphere. One joke played on the oc-
casional jibes against "reactionaries" found in Nazi propaganda:

*Question: What is a reactionary? Answer: Someone who
occupies a well-paying job coveted by a Nazi.*

Similar in thrust, although somewhat more original, was another
popular quip:

*A cook is trying to make fried potatoes without lard and be-
gins waving a swastika banner over the oven. When asked
why, she answers: "Under this flag, a lot of lard-asses seem
to have come out pretty well."*

One Nazi bigwig who was especially crass about taking what he
wanted was Foreign Minister Joachim von Ribbentrop. In 1939,
after the annexation of Austria, von Ribbentrop took a fancy to
the idyllic Fuschl Castle and simply dispossessed its owner, Gustav Edler von Remiz. This forced entry into the landed nobility
earned him the nickname "von Ribbensnob."

The crude behavior of Ribbentrop and other fascist officials
upset the German populace far more than the brutal Nazi pogroms. Popular doubts about the party were expressed in a political joke that turned on two meanings of the German word
wählen: "to dial a telephone number" and "to vote for someone":

*The telephone rings, and a man says: "Hello, can I speak to
Müller?" "Who?" "Müller. Is Müller there?" "No, my name
is Schmidt." "Oh, I'm sorry, I must have dialed the wrong
person." "No big deal, we all did that in the last election."*

Hitler himself had not been directly elected, but as the leader of the party that came out best in the general elections he had been charged by President Paul von Hindenburg with forming a coalition to take over state power. Nonetheless, in the early days of the Third Reich, there was no significant anti-Hitler opposition. On the contrary, historical contemporaries consistently remember the time prior to World War II as the "good years" of Nazism, the period in which unemployment declined and Germans began to feel confident again after a decade of deep insecurity and depression. Such an attitude may appear cynical now, considering that along with the economic upswing came an increasing number of government strictures, the rapid dismantling of civil rights, and violent suppression of the opposition. Nevertheless, an extraordinary number of people felt that that things had changed for the better.

The noticeable improvement in the economy and the youthful optimism the Nazis spread obscured the dark side of the regime. In addition, Hitler knew how to portray his own ruthless grasp for power, which extended to the most insignificant office, as a "national uprising." There was virtually no public resistance to the bright future that was constantly being trumpeted by the Ministry of Propaganda. The ideological techniques Joseph Goebbels used to blind the German populace were effective. It took Mussolini seven years to amass the sort of power in Italy that the Nazis were able to grab in Germany in mere months. The remaining parliamentary structures quickly collapsed, in part because they lacked popular support to begin with. People on the street suppressed any unease they might have felt at Hitler's rapid and brutal seizure of power and told themselves it was no use going against the tide. Individual Germans repressed concerns about, or simply ignored, the terrible consequences awaiting many of their fellow citizens. They were more concerned with establishing their own place in the new Aryan racial community.

Tellingly, in the months after Hitler came to power, the ranks of the Nazi party swelled. People from across the political spectrum ended traditional allegiances and joined the NSDAP, and conversions from Communism were particularly frequent. Both Hitler himself and the populace took bemused note of the numbers of so-called March violets, latecomers to the Nazi party. One popular joke ran:

> [Nazi Labor Minister] Ley visits a factory and, after taking a tour, he asks the director about political views among his work force. "Do you still have any Social Democrats?" "Yes, around 80 percent." "What about Centrists?" "Sure, around 20 percent." "But that means you don't have any National Socialists?" "Of course we do. They're all Nazis now."

In general, jokes from the early years of the Third Reich amounted to little more than harmless teasing of the regime and could be told in public without fear of reprisals. "We weren't anxious," recalls Carl-Ludwig Schulz from Berlin, who lived through the period. "But there was a kind of political correctness in Germany, and it began leading to concrete acts of oppression once the war started."

JOKES THAT TOUCHED upon Nazi brutality were very unusual. It was much more common for Germans to laugh at Nazi habits and customs, which had their ridiculous side. One prominent example was the Nazi insistence on the "German greeting," the raised-arm salute that Hitler had copied from the

Italian fascists. Nazi propagandists never tired of encouraging
Germans to demonstrate their loyalty in this way. "When you as.
a German enter a place," the slogan of one such campaign ran,
"your first words should be 'Heil Hitler!'" Only the most ardent
Nazis felt comfortable using the new greeting, but it was quickly
made mandatory for all public buildings and all government situations. The people of Cologne soon came up with a joke concerning the ritual, using two figures from local folklore, Tünnes and
Schäl:

> *Tünnes and Schäl are walking across a cow pasture, when
> Tünnes steps in a mound of cowshit and almost falls down.
> Immediately he raises his right arm and yells, "Heil Hit-
> ler!" "Are you crazy?" asks Schäl. "What are you doing?
> There's no one else around here." "I'm following regulations,"
> Tünnes answers. "Whenever you step into anywhere, you're
> supposed to say 'Heil Hitler.'"*

But the intentions behind the greeting were no laughing matter.
The salute and the words "Heil Hitler" were a litmus test by which
Nazis could find out whether someone was an ally or a potential enemy. Former Social Democrats or Communists were not
always enthusiastic about making the bizarre gesture, but those
who failed to do so could face serious consequences. In one case,
the authorities took a child away from his parents after he had
repeatedly failed to give the greeting in school. That, however,
was in 1940, when political tensions had already been ratcheted
up and Germans had gotten used to the custom. In the early years
of the Reich, most people still found it unsettling and made it a
mainstay of political humor. One joke suggested that as long as
Germans ran around saying "Heil Hitler," there weren't going to

be any more "good days"—since the greeting "Heil Hitler" re-placed the more typical "good day." One of the funnier jokes of the time was the following:

> *Hitler visits a lunatic asylum, where the patients all duti-fully perform the German salute. Suddenly, Hitler sees one man whose arm is not raised. "Why don't you greet me the same way as everyone else," he hisses. The man answers: "My Führer, I'm an orderly, not a madman!"*

Less amusing were jokes punning on the two meanings of the word *heil*: "hail" and "heal." In one of them, a doctor at another asylum, responds to "Heil Hitler!" with "Heal him yourself!"

Many jokes about the greeting used the same pun. The fol-lowing joke (mistakenly ascribed to Munich comedian Karl Val-entin) is one:

> *A drunkard passes a vendor on the street who is crying, "Heilkräuter!"("Medicinal herbs!"). "Heil Kräuter?" he pon-ders. "We must have a new government."*

The many parodies of the "German greeting" may have allowed those who did not identify all that closely with Nazi ideology to avoid using the offending original phrase. It was common to say "Drei Liter" ("three liters") when entering bars or to elide "Heil Hitler" into "Heitler." The most original parody came from a group of young men who called themselves "Swing Kids;" they rebelled against the spirit of the time by growing their hair long and listening to swing, which the Nazis rejected as "nigger mu-sic." They greeted one another with the words "Swing heil!" And because the German greeting was actually an Italian import, one joke had Il Duce greeting Der Führer on a state visit with the words "Ave, Copycat."

Perhaps the best takeoff on the Hitler greeting, however, was that of a performer from Paderborn: he taught his trained chimpanzees to extend their arms in Nazi fashion. (According to the performer's son, the chimpanzees enjoyed doing this.) Every time the animals saw someone in uniform, even a postman, they would give the Nazi salute. This dadaistic coup of the Paderborn comic, who was a committed Social Democrat, attracted the ire of his "racial comrades," who reported him to the authorities. A directive was soon issued forbidding apes from using the Hitler greeting, with the penalty for noncompliance being the "slaughter" of the animals. When it came to expressions of respect for their leader, the Nazis did not have much sense of humor.

ON FEBRUARY 27, 1933, a catastrophic fire destroyed the Reichstag, and the Nazi leadership recognized the event as an opportunity, which they proceeded to exploit with instinctive assurance. It was the beginning of the process by which the Nazis silenced their political opponents and destroyed the democratic system. Göring was the first Nazi leader at the site of the fire; Hitler arrived shortly thereafter. While the remains of the building were still smoldering, the two decided to blame the disaster on the Communists and Social Democrats: they would claim the blaze had been set deliberately, as the first act of an incipient left-wing revolt.

In fact, political blunders by their leadership and their declining popularity with the masses had so weakened the German Communists that they could hardly have mounted an effective nationwide resistance to the Nazi regime. But Göring and Hitler weren't interested in distinctions between real and imaginary threats. They alertly seized the moment and had some 4,000 Communist functionaries arrested, including the party's leader, Ernst Thälmann. They also struck out at opposition writers, doctors, and lawyers. The morning after the fire, Hitler appeared before the aged Paul von Hindenburg and painted a most melodramatic picture of the situation. Cowed by the chancellor's Grand Guignol scenario, the last president of the Weimar Republic signed the Enabling Act, making Hitler virtual dictator and effectively terminating the rights guaranteed by the Weimar constitution. Under this emergency rule, the government could order arrests at will and was freed from any legal checks and balances. The use of the death penalty was expanded, and the government was charged to ensure "order" and "security" wherever necessary, a provision that curtailed the rights of the individual local states that made up Germany and created a monolithic central authority.

The speed and efficiency with which the Nazis enacted their measures after the Reichstag fire has perennially given rise to speculation about who the real arsonists had been. After World War II, there were persistent rumors that Göring himself had ordered the blaze, and even directly after the fire, many Germans entertained similar suspicions. What people believed had less to do with the few available hard facts of the case than with individuals' own political views. The same was true of the foreign press. Some foreign journalists immediately accused the Nazis of having set the fire themselves, while others simply chronicled the controversy about the identity of the true culprit.

The Nazis eventually blamed a Dutch Communist, a confused and partially blind man named Marinus van der Lubbe. But few of those who were critical of the Nazi-led government believed that van der Lubbe, using only a handful of household fire starters, could have ignited the fire that destroyed such a massive structure. "Eight days before the election, and then a crass stunt like the Reichstag fire," wrote Viktor Klemperer in his diary. "I can't imagine anyone believes in Communist culprits instead of a contract job commissioned on behalf of the swastika." And another contemporary, Rolf Rothe, noted, "This young fellow van der Lubbe, how could he alone have ignited the Reichstag? No person could have caused such a massive stone building to burst into flames! No one believed that. It would have been completely absurd!"

The mystery surrounding the Reichstag fire was perfect fodder for comedians. Before long, people were circulating countless jokes that unmistakably, if with varying comic success, played upon the idea that the Nazi themselves had caused the fire.

These jokes fell into two groups. The first group blamed the SA and the SS, which many Germans hated and feared, for the catastrophe. One such joke involved a pun on the letter *S*, a homonym for *Ess*, German for the familiar imperative "Eat!":

A father and his son are sitting at the dinner table. The son asks: "Papa, who started the Reichstag fire?" The father answers: "Ess, ess [SS], and quit asking so many questions."

Other jokes in this vein took the form of riddles:

Q. Who set fire to the Reichstag?
A. The brothers Sass [SA+SS].

Q. What's the different between a regular army and an SA unit?
A. In the army they say, "Ready, get set, fire!" In the SA they say, "Get ready and set fire!"

The second group of jokes assigned the blame not to Nazi thugs, but rather to Göring himself. There were a number of good reasons why he was singled out. He was known as a man of immediate and cold-blooded action. As state premier of Prussia, he also controlled the executive branch of government, of which he made ample, unscrupulous use. But in the show trials after the fire, aimed at exposing the "Communist plot," Göring's appearances were so clumsy that people began to doubt his honesty. One of the accused Communists, Georgi Dimitrow, mounted a vigorous defense, and his eloquence repeatedly forced Göring into a verbal corner. In the end, the Communists were acquitted—a serious embarrassment for the Nazi leadership.

The trial let the genie out of its bottle, and the Nazis had no means of containing it. During the proceedings, Dimitrow had voiced the suspicion that the Nazis had started the fire themselves, and since the trial was being broadcast live on radio, there was no way such statements could be simply suppressed. Doubts concerning Göring's role in the blaze were brought directly into Germans' living rooms and became the subject of a variety of witticisms:

On the evening of February 27, Göring's assistant arrives out of breath at his boss's office and yells, "State Premier Göring, the Reichstag is on fire!" Göring looks at the clock, shakes his head in surprise, and says, "What, already?"

"Yesterday, Göring was seen in Leipzig Street." "Really? Where was the fire?"

Time has destroyed much of the evidence, and witnesses' testimony was contradictory, so there is no way of knowing whether

Göring really was responsible for the destruction of the Reichstag. We can assume that neither Hitler nor Goebbels planned the arson, since both reacted with shock when they heard the news that the building was in flames. In light of the most current research, the most probable, if also least spectacular, scenario is that van der Lubbe did indeed set the fire on his own.

There is little reason to believe that any political party contracted him to do so. The Communists had no motivation, and there is no hard evidence of Nazi involvement. What is clear is that from February 27, 1933, onward, the SA and Göring, who occupied one of the highest offices in the German government, were surrounded by ugly suspicions that were kept alive in innumerable jokes. Nonetheless, despite their anger at the outcome of the show trials and the damage to their own reputation, thanks to the fire the Nazis had taken a decisive step toward consolidating their rule. The party was able to maintain the pretence that Hitler had accrued power by entirely legal means, even as it dismantled the Weimar Constitution, and to generally rely upon the maxim that never is a people more ready to accept injustice than at the beginning of a new dictatorship.

IN THE MONTHS following Hitler's assumption of extraordinary power, the Nazis were assiduous in eradicating the protections offered by the German legal system. Their goal was to see all of society brought into line with Nazi ideology, if not voluntarily then forcibly. One of the first steps was the ordinance "For the Protection of the German People," issued on February 4, 1933, allowing the new government to ban publications and assemblies by their political opponents. Hitler warned journalists against making "mistakes" in their reporting, accompanying the warnings with the direst threats of what would happen if they failed to do so. Other measures followed, one after another. The red, black, and gold flag of the Weimar Republic was replaced by the swastika, and the federal structure of Germany was abolished by decree.

The Nazis were particularly unscrupulous about eradicating hubs of local power and centralizing political authority. In Bavaria, Himmler and SA chief of staff Ernst Röhm forced the local state premier to step down, and Göring took violent measures against anyone who opposed the "national uprising" the Nazis were propagating. The speed with which events were proceeding, the increasing license enjoyed by the SA, the combination of patriotic agitation and naked brutality had the desired effect on the German populace. The new regime presented two faces: one euphoric and one dark and threatening. Those who were proof against fascist enthusiasm were systematically bullied into submission. That inspired the following witticism, playing on *braun,* German for "brown"—the color associated with the SA—and *schweigen,* "to remain silent":

> *Since all the federal states have been brought into line, we are once again one people. There are no longer any Prussians, Bavarian, Thuringians, or Saxons. Instead, we're all Braunschweigers.*

The punch line gained extra pungency from the fact that the city of Braunschweig had elected a Nazi local government very early, in September 1930, and had indeed given Hitler, who was born in Austria, German citizenship. Naturalization, of course, had been a key prerequisite for Hitler becoming German chancellor.

From the beginning, Braunschweig's fascist rulers had played a crucial role not only in the party's rise to national power but also in its attempt to bring the Protestant Church into its fold. The Weimar Republic had secularized the German state. State subsidies to churches had been reduced, and in many parts of Germany religion no longer played a dominant role in the schools. That had angered many German clergy. The Nazi government in Braunschweig reintroduced school prayers and paid outstanding subsidies. Those policies had their desired effect. One third of Protestant clergymen in Braunschweig joined the Nazi party, and before long the cross and swastika were blazoned side by side on church publications.

After assuming power on the national level, the Nazi leadership continued and even expanded such church-friendly policies. Official acts of state always featured religious trappings, and Hitler never tired in his speeches of thanking God for his newly acquired power. This was little more than maneuvering, of course, to get the church in step with Nazi ideology, but such masterpieces of propaganda paid long dividends. Some pastors even began appearing in the pulpit wearing brown shirts and jackboots. Skeptics had once joked: "Hitler is powerless against incense (religion) and garlic (supposed Jewish influence)." Hitler, however, proved them wrong.

The Protestant Church was hardly a monolithic institution, and a schism soon opened up between the Nazi "German Christians," led by a Protestant pastor named Ludwig Müller, and the opposition "Emergency Association of Pastors," led by Martin Niemöller. Müller, a personal acquaintance of Hitler, was appointed Imperial Bishop. He wasn't known for his intellectual prowess and was certainly no match for his opponents from the traditional church, particularly Niemöller. He was given a number of unflattering popular nicknames and became the butt of a host of more or less successful jokes:

> *When Goebbels published his book* From the Imperial Court to the German Chancellery, *the Imperial Bishop couldn't rest until he'd written a work of his own. The title was:* From Leading Light to Dim Bulb.

Another quip from the time was that the Imperial Bishop had such thick skin he didn't need a backbone. Despite Müller's shortcomings as the head of the "German Christians," the Nazis reached an arrangement with both Catholic and Protestant churches, although threats were still constantly needed to ensure that no one disturbed this artificial harmony.

Clerics who were critical of the regime enjoyed sympathy among the populace, since they were the only ones in society left after the initial period of purges and bullying who continued to represent an alternative system of belief to Nazism. One joke praised the Catholic bishop of Münster, Count Clemens August von Galen:

> *In one of his sermons, Count von Galen criticized the educational programs of the Hitler Youth. A member of the congregation interrupted him: "How can a man without children dare to speak about education?" Von Galen countered, "Sir, I'm not going to tolerate any criticism of our Führer in my church."*

Von Galen earned the nickname "the Lion of Münster" for his fearless resistance against Nazi educational policies and euthanasia programs. Germans admired him for taking a stand, despite the risk of retribution, against the murder of retarded persons, a policy that outraged many people at the time. A Nazi ministerial counselor tried to justify the program by arguing that the commandment "Thou shalt not kill" had been not the word of God but rather "a Jewish invention" aimed at "denying their enemies an effective defense in order to dispose of them all the more easily."

Von Galen survived the Third Reich, but countless other clergymen were killed in what was known as the "pastors' block" of the Dachau concentration camp. The persecution of men of the cloth who criticized the regime may have inspired a number of satirical riffs on religious holidays. Examples include "Maria Incarcerata" and "Maria Denunciata." The Latin of the Lord's Prayer was also parodied, with the line "et ne nos inducas temptationem" (lead us not into temptation) changed to "et ne nos inducas concentrationem"—a clear reference to the concentration camps.

The crimes the Nazis committed during the Third Reich were only possible because the German courts had also been brought into line. In 1935, authority over the judicial system was transferred from the federal states to the central government. As soon as they seized power, the Nazis began systematically preparing German lawyers and judges, traditionally a conservative lot, to function in a state not based on the rule of law. The Association of National Socialist Attorneys trained young judges, prosecutors, and defense lawyers. The new doctrine of the German legal system was that judgments should be rendered in the interests of the government, and there was no need to stick too closely to laws. "The healthy opinion of the people" was elevated above legal guarantees, the phrase *healthy opinion* serving to whitewash the justice that the fascists meted out as they pleased. At least some German citizens watched in consternation as the Nazis ran roughshod over the German constitution—a concern reflected in the sardonic rumor that the following laws were about to be decreed:

§1 Anyone who does something or fails to do something will be punished.
§2 Punishment will be handed down according to popular opinion.
§3 Popular opinion is defined by the Nazi district leader [Gauleiter].

Indeed, some people during the Third Reich wondered why the government felt it needed a legal system at all. Right from the start, there were crass cases of injustice, and measures taken to terrorize enemies were both extreme and arbitrary.

One joke played on this very point, and its punch line had a twisted logic:

> *A high-ranking Nazi official visiting Switzerland asks what a certain public building is for. "That's our Navy Ministry," his Swiss host explains. The Nazi laughs and says: "Why does Switzerland need a ministry of the navy? You've only got two or three ships." The Swiss answers, "Why not? Germany has a ministry of justice."*

Yet even in the final stage of World War II, even while they murdered thousands of Jews every day in Eastern Europe, the Nazis were unwilling to do without the pretence of legality, for instance in the form of judgments handed down by the notorious People's Court. In 1933, the Nazis were already thinking in terms of what Hitler called a "legal revolution" and began laying the groundwork of their new system for administering injustice. Laws were constantly issued that turned German citizens into arbitrary victims of state authorities. As early as February 28, 1933, they adopted their infamous idea of "protective custody"—a concept that allowed them to incarcerate their political opponents without trial. The basic judicial principle, cynics joked, was now brutality before legality.

The Nazification of the government, the church, and the judicial system was accompanied by fascist purges of Germany's cultural edifice as well. Within the first few months of Hitler's assumption of absolute political power, Goebbels claimed similar authority over culture through his newly created Ministry of Propaganda. Anyone who wished to work in Germany as a writer, an artist, or an actor was required to join the Reich Chamber of Culture or one of its subordinate organizations. Those who remained outside or were excluded from this state association were effectively prohibited from working. Moreover, the Nazis didn't handle artists they considered a nuisance with kid gloves. By the spring of 1933, some 250 well-known German authors, including Thomas Mann, Lion Feuchtwanger, and Stefan Zweig, had been stripped of their citizenship and the works of "enemy" writers were being publicly burned, in theatrical spectacles featuring bizarre "campfire speeches" by Nazi agitators. Meanwhile, instead of voicing their opposition to the book burnings, other prominent cultural figures, like the actor Gustav Gründgens and the writer Gerhart Hauptmann and including, sometimes, even personal friends of the persecuted writers, were pledging their fealty to their new leaders. Behind closed doors, many of these artists may have complained about the banal monotony of the "Pitiful Chamber of Culture," but most of them simply adapted to the times.

Goebbels was equally eager to achieve a quick and smooth Nazification of the German press. Opposition newspapers were banned, and others were forced out of business by state subsidies handed out to rivals. The Ministry of Propaganda took care to ensure that some semblance of journalistic variety remained, but only in layout and appearance—not in the centrally dictated, strictly nationalistic content of the articles.

As strange as it might seem today, many Germans at the time actually applauded the eradication of the free press. The Munich cabaret performer and early Nazi sympathizer Weiß Ferdl, for example, wrote a song praising Nazification and comparing it to the Nazi campaigns against jazz and other forms of "nigger music." The text might read like a parody today, but during the Third Reich it was sung without irony. Its "humor" consisted of a play on *Gleichschaltung* (literally, "same-keeping"), the German term for bringing everything into line with Nazi interests and ideology:

> *There used to be so many parties,*
> *And also a lot of friction*
> *Until an engineer spoke his opinion:*
> *No, dear Germans, this can't go on,*
> *No more alternating currents—*
> *A single one will do just fine.*
> *He converted some and turned off others,*
> *And brought everything into line.*
>
> *It used to be that reading papers*
> *Made you stupid and even crazy.*
> *One wrote "Bravo! Very good!"*
> *Another "Pfui!" The truth stayed hazy.*
> *Now you can save your dime,*
> *If you've read one, you know what's right,*
> *They say the same thing every time,*
> *Brought into line, brought into line.*

We no longer like the saxophone
We don't dance the rumba or the Charleston
No more jazz or nigger steps,
We've stopped playing the simpleton,
We hear the songs of yesteryear
Marching music, German rhyme,
And they are pleasant to the ear,
Brought into line, brought into line.

If a man wants a second woman
And can't stay true to his wife,
A German lady, she can threaten
To send him to Dachau for life.
"For twenty years you did enjoy
All my charms, and that was fine,
And so it will be—you, too, are older,"
Brought into line, brought into line.

At meetings for disarmament,
Frenchmen never stopped complaining
"Germany poses us all a threat,"
But the world's no longer listening.
Our chancellor spoke an open word:
"Only he can say peace is mine
Who destroys his weapons and keeps his word,"
Brought into line, brought into line.

United are Prussians and Bavarians
And won't be parted ever again.
Instead to going to the mountains
Let's spend a weekend in Berlin.

We'll go sledding in Luna Park
While the Prussians learn to yodel fine.
Boy, do we now stick together,
Brought into line, brought into line.

And if we strongly stick together,
Everything will be looking great
For farmer, worker, and every servant
Noble or common, the same good fate.
In the land that we fought for
And suffered years of pain,
We now want to live together,
Brought into line, brought into line.

Ferdl wrote these verses the year after Hitler became chancellor, and they are one of the many examples of cultural figures declaring their loyalty to the Nazis in those early days.

During that period, however, some people still resisted Nazification. Many respectable middle-class citizens shook their heads at the Nazis' provocative, drastically anti-Semitic publications. But there was little significant revolt among the Germans, who considered themselves a people of "thinkers and poets," as the Nazis set about remaking the German press and German culture in their own image. Their resistance extended only to hiding the works of the great German-Jewish writers in the second rows of their bookshelves, and perhaps allowing themselves a small sarcastic joke in private about the banality of Nazi culture. One sadly untranslatable example of such a joke revolves around a schoolteacher having his pupils practice comparatives and superlatives using three Nazi newspapers. In the punch line, one pupil responds that *Der Stürmer*, the virulently anti-Semitic organ of the SA, is at its best when applied most intimately—that is, used to wipe one's ass. The pattern of the joke is typical for the Nazi years: the punch line is a naïve, unthinking remark put into the mouth of a child, a circumstance that takes some of the sting out of an insult aimed at Nazi culture and would have allowed the joke-teller to protest his innocence, if accused of fomenting political discontent.

In the first years of the Third Reich, German society was not only Nazified but militarized. The Nazis created numerous and, in part, competing organizations in which people from all walks of life and of all ages were required to appear in uniform. The result was a Kafkaesque confusion of official garb on German streets shortly after Hitler took power. That gave rise to the popular quip that soldiers would soon have to wear civilian clothing to distinguish themselves from the masses.

The spread of Nazism also meant the absurd spread of acronyms for the often clumsy names of Nazi organizations, which included not just the SS and SA, but also the BDM (Association of German Girls), the HJ (Hitler Youth), and the NSKK (National Socialist Corps of Auto Mechanics). The explosion in abbreviations quickly became the subject of mostly harmless jokes:

> *The number of organizations continues to expand. Before they are eligible for the SS and SA, young people are recruited to the HJ, the younger ones to the Jungvolk, and those younger still to Nazi kindergartens. Now infants are being organized. They are called T.U.R.D. Scouts.*

Jokes like this didn't aim any serious criticism at the paramilitary nature of Nazi organizations. At most, such witticisms targeted the disruptions to normal family life party duties entailed:

My father is a SA man, my oldest brother is in the SS, my little brother is a member of the HJ, my mother belongs to the Nazi Women's Group, and I'm in the BDM. We meet up once a year at the Nuremberg Rallies.

The acronym BDM in particular was fodder for sexual jokes, with the abbreviation being made to stand for "Soon-to-be German Mothers," "Commodities for German Men" or "Boy, Mount Me." As was typical for the period, these jokes had no pointed political thrust and can hardly be interpreted as signs of a basic skepticism among the populace toward the regime.

GERMANS ENJOYED laughing at the bizarre particulars of National Socialism, but the new system, despite some initial criticism, was soon firmly anchored in German society. And as a gesture of gratitude, the regime repaid the populace with instances of seeming liberalness. The Nazis were apparently worried that they would be seen as thickheaded thugs with no sense of humor, and occasionally policies were aimed at communicating the message that the party leaders weren't as fearsome as their reputations. One of the strangest results of this charm offensive was a compilation of foreign anti-Hitler caricatures that was published in Germany in 1933. The editor of the fancily bound volume was none other than the Nazi responsible for dealing with the foreign press, Hitler's boyhood friend Ernst "Putzi" Hanfstaengl.

In his introduction, Hanfstaengl wrote:

The mocking, distorted images used by a degenerate press to depict Adolf Hitler as he fulfills his historic mission are reminiscent of cacophonous jazz music. The naysayers and defamers are shamefully unmasked by their own work.... The value of this compilation of caricatures of the Führer resides in the fact that they, more than any other opposing voices, argue for him. Every image reveals how wrongly the world has seen and judged Adolf Hitler. Those who study the book attentively will get a good laugh at every picture, not because the caricaturists are so witty, but because they have gotten things so obviously wrong.

In fact, Hanfstaengl did not trust his readership to draw the correct conclusions. To ensure that readers laughed at the right things for the right reasons, Hanfstaengl added propagandistic glosses to the caricatures.

For instance, one image from *The Nation* depicted Hitler as a grim reaper with an army of skeletons marching at his feet. The reaper's scythe was shaped like a swastika, and its blades dripped with blood. On the following page, Hanfstaengl interpreted the picture for his readers:

The press: The image suggests Hitler is a warmonger.

The facts: On July 15, 1933, Hitler authorized the German ambassador in Rome to sign the Four Powers' Pact, through which England, France, Italy, and Germany ensured peace in Europe for the next ten years.

Another caricature in the compilation portrayed Hitler as a fearsome Indian chief with an enemy's head impaled on a spear. The caption read: "The chief of a savage tribe after the Battle of Leipzig and in full war dress." Hanfstaengl's gloss:

The press: On September 25, 1930, Hitler testified before a Leipzig court that "heads would roll" when the Nazis took power in Germany.

The facts: After taking power, Hitler did indeed cause a number of heads to "roll" into the concentration camps. This was because he had decided to be a generous victor and because he wished to spare the healthy productive masses of the German people from a bloody confrontation with their enemies.

Hanfstaengl's "corrections" could hardly have been more cynical, but the fascist press applauded his machinations. In the publicity blurb on the book jacket, a director of nature films, Luis Trenker, wrote that Hanfstaengl's work would "recall to our minds the heroically pursued struggle of our Führer."

Hanfstaengel's declaration of loyalty to Hitler went for nothing. In 1937, he was forced to flee to America after a conflict with Goebbels. The man who had tried to stir up hatred against Jews and the Nazis' political enemies became a *persona non grata* in the Third Reich. But his career continued. Franklin Roosevelt used him as a political and psychological adviser during World War II. In 1946, after the demise of the Nazi regime, Hanfstaengel returned to Germany and wrote his memoirs. He died there in 1975, without ever having been called to answer for his past.

A tragic destiny, on the other hand, awaited a man who had turned against the Nazis voluntarily, and much sooner. The caricaturist Erich Ohser, who was born in 1903, attracted the displeasure of the Nazis early in the 1930s after he published a number of satirical depictions of Hitler. One showed a man out for a walk in the snow urinating in the form of a swastika. Another image merged Hitler's moustache and hairstyle into a frightening grimace that cast the Führer as a warmonger. Ohser's courage would not go unpunished. When he later applied for membership in the Imperial Chamber of Culture he was rejected and couldn't get any work. The letter he received from the chamber on January 17, 1934, read: "On the basis of your earlier, explicitly Marxist public work, the Commission of the Regional Press Association of Berlin has decided negatively regarding your request for acceptance into the expert committee of journalistic illustrators in the Imperial Association of the German Press and for entry into its professional rolls." Seized by panic, Ohser burned the originals of drawings he had done for the left-wing newspaper *Vorwärts*, but to no avail. His anti-Nazi caricatures had appeared in mass circulation, and Goebbels and his henchmen could hardly be expected to forget his earlier criticisms of fascism.

Gritting his teeth, Ohser adapted to the times, at least externally, and began publishing apolitical cartoons under the pseudonym E. O. Plauen. His series *Father and Son* enjoyed enormous popularity, and that opened doors to the newspaper *Das Reich*, which was considered relatively liberal. There, he sold a number of political cartoons that were careful not to overstep fascist lines. Ohser drew anti-British and anti-Soviet caricatures, but in his private life he made no secret of his real political convictions. In the next-to-last year of World War II, this personal frankness undid him. A neighbor reported anti-Nazi remarks made in a conversation between Ohser and his friend Erich Knauf, and the two men were hauled up in front of the People's Court. Ohser committed suicide before the trial; Knauf was executed in May 1944.

THE CABARET ARTIST Werner Finck had far better luck than Ohser. Nazi prosecutors ignored him for an astonishingly long time, although the courageous comedian became an underground hit in the early Hitler era for his risky political jokes. Finck had a standing engagement at the Berlin cabaret house Catacomb. This small theater became something of a legend in postwar Germany, but despite its later reputation, Catacomb was not strictly a venue for political cabaret. Instead, it put on variety shows that featured sketches and small-stage acts. A chanson singer usually appeared, and then a mime, before Finck took the stage. One could say that he was responsible for the political segment of a general entertainment. Indeed, some artists who worked in the Catacomb in the early 1930s considered it too apolitical and founded a harder-hitting cabaret house of their own.

Those artists were forced into exile after Hitler's assumption of power, while Finck became a master of ambiguity. His performances were famous for what they *didn't* say. Every one of his appearances was a dance on a knife's edge. Finck knew that if his criticism of the regime became too explicit, the Nazis would ban his act, label him a political enemy, and send him to a concentration camp. He was forced to adopt a number of tricks in order to conceal political messages in harmless packaging. His audiences knew the point of Finck's game, and the comedian's daring verbal acrobatics gave his act an additional appeal. The kick one got was similar to watching a high-wire artist working without a net. People thrilled to the danger and laughed because they were able to read between the lines. Finck himself accurately described the situation when he said that during the Third Reich, one only had to strike a tiny bell with a tiny hammer to create a deafening uproar, whereas later you could hit a giant bell with a giant hammer and only a tiny sound would come out. Germans under Hitler were highly sensitized and could tell when invisible boundaries were being crossed.

Finck, the master of humorous transgressions, was also a sly operator. In 1933, for instance, he founded the seemingly innocent "Fighting Association for Harmless Humor" (KfhH), an organization whose name sounded well in Nazi ears. In the Catacomb's program, the "Association" published the following Finck verses:

A fresh wind is blowing
We want to laugh again
Humor, awaken!
We'll give you free rein.

While the lion is crowned
And Mars rules the hour
Good cheer, which we all love,
Is slowly turning sour.

Let's not allow the devil
Or any other powers
To rob us of the fun
That is rightfully ours.

Let the power of words
Vibrate the eardrums
And if anyone objects, he can
Kiss us on our bums.

These lines were full parodies of Nazi slogans, such as "Germany, awaken!," and authorities intervened and banned the program. Finck's rhyming takeoff on Nazi jargon prodded the Nazis in what was apparently a sore spot. But in the pseudo-tolerant years of the early Third Reich a modicum of criticism was tolerated. Indeed, the Nazis occasionally had some kind words for Finck. In a review of a Catacomb spring show, published in the Nazi party's chief organ, the *Völkischer Beobachter*, an adjutant to Propaganda Minister Goebbels praised the performer for his "witty joking and sometimes surprising punch lines." And the editor-in-chief of *Der Angriff*, which was published by Goebbels himself, wrote in the Catacomb's visitor's book: "Dangerous or not—keep going!"

Later, in the 1960s, Finck related an anecdote that summed up the absurdity of situation in the supposedly liberal era of the early Third Reich. One evening he was approached by a man in civilian clothing. After some hemming and hawing, the man revealed that he was an officer in the SA. The man invited Finck to visit his office, saying that they could tell politically incorrect jokes there and have a lot of fun. The offer was meant completely ingenuously, although Finck, understandably, declined.

The surprising instances of tolerance and the friendly remarks quickly came to an end. The propagandistic display of liberalism in the initial months after Hitler assumed power was just a step toward achieving the Nazis' overall homicidal plan. Initially, the regime was careful to present a lenient face, especially to the rest of the world. The screws, however, would soon be tightened and the comedian from the Catacomb left staring into the abyss.

ONE OF THE MOST portentous things the National Socialists did in the months following the Reichstag fire was to set up the first concentration camps in Germany. The paradigm of the camps was Dachau, near Munich. Set up in March 1933 under the direction of a sadistic commandant named Theodor Eiche, it rapidly achieved a tragic notoriety well beyond Bavaria. At first, Communists, union activists, and Social Democrats were the prisoners most frequently interred and occasionally tortured there. However, they were soon joined by Sinti and Roma, Jews, Jehovah's Witnesses, homosexuals, and common criminals. Dachau was never an extermination camp like Auschwitz. Nonetheless, over the years thousands of people died there—shot or tortured to death.

In the early days of the Reich, the Nazis kept up the pretence that Dachau was a "re-education camp" and that people confined there could hope to be released some day. But it was an open secret that the camp was actually an extralegal space in which torture and murder were allowed. Contemporaries relate that it was common for parents to tell misbehaving children that they would be sent to Dachau if they didn't shape up. But the public outrage that should have arisen at this example of state terror never materialized. One man, Fritz Muliar, recalls that photos of Dachau were published in Austria in 1937 showing inmates with head wounds. Germans suspected the true dimension of the crimes that were being perpetrated at Dachau, but seeing them, and believing their eyes, would have required action. The public's reaction to Dachau was silence. Germans kept their mouths shut and looked the other way.

The name of Dachau became shorthand for the entire network of concentration camps—as illustrated by its prominence in the jokes of the time. An only half satirical prayer made the rounds: "Dear God, please make me silent and repent so that I don't get to Dachau sent." But many Dachau jokes seem to have been aimed more at accustoming Germans to this new phenomenon than articulating any real criticism of it. The following joke was attributed to Nazi sympathizer Weiß Ferdl:

I took an excursion to Dachau, and boy what a place it is! Barbed wire, machine guns, barbed wire, more machine guns, and then more barbed wire. But I tell you: Nonetheless, if I want to, I'll get in.

It is ironic that Ferdl, who used to open the bill for Hitler's speeches when the Führer was still a relatively unknown agitator, was sometimes credited with anti-Nazi jokes. Though the cabaret performer sometimes allowed himself an equivocal remark, his political orientation was beyond doubt. His reputation as an adversary of Hitler was undeserved and was probably owed to his audience misinterpreting ambiguous passages in his songs.

But there was no need for even a Nazi loyalist to be enigmatic about Dachau, which was never mistaken for a sanatorium. The variety of popular idioms and jokes featuring Dachau as a concentration camp belies many Germans' assertions after World War II that they didn't know what was going on there. The following joke, for example, absolutely depends on the hearer's assumption that a concentration camp is an extralegal realm where prisoners are terrorized and a place where one can be sent at any time for criticizing the Nazi regime:

Two men meet up on the street, and the first one says: "Nice to see you out again. How was the concentration camp?"

The second man replies, "It was great. Mornings we got breakfast in bed, with our choice of freshly ground coffee or cocoa. We did some sports, and then there was a three-course lunch with soup, meat, and dessert. After that we played some board games and took a nap. And after dinner, they showed movies."

The first man can't believe his ears. "Wow! And the

lies they spread about the place. Recently I was talking to Meyer, who also spent some time there. He told me horror stories."

The second man nods seriously and says, "That's why he got sent back."

This joke makes clear that even in the early days of the Third Reich, Germans were afraid that if they said the wrong thing they'd be arrested and sent to a place like Dachau. Thus the danger of humor itself quickly became the subject of humor:

Whaddaya got for new jokes?
Three months in Dachau.

Such jesting, ironically, is evidence that the concentration camps, along with emergency ordinances allowing things like "protective custody," were indeed the effective deterrent to free speech—including free humorous speech—that they were intended to be.

After the Reichstag fire, Germany was kept in a permanent state of emergency to justify the government's exercise of autocratic powers. The Nazis argued that "enemies of the state" could not be stopped using the regular instruments of the Weimar judicial system and with this excuse stacked the deck against those they accused of treasonous activities. There was no appeal against the decisions of the special courts the Nazis introduced, and those merely under suspicion were hardly safe, for suspect persons could be held without charge. The Gestapo, which acted independently from the regular Nazi legal system, was empowered to detain people for whatever reason and for however long it deemed fit. Those who were released from protective custody bore the stigma of being criminals, and other Germans avoided them as if they carried a contagious disease. Government authorities rendered decisions about what behavior was permitted or forbidden more or less arbitrarily.

Most of the laws the Nazis enacted were little more than pseudo-legal window-dressing. On March 21, 1933, the "Ordinance of the Imperial President for the Defense against Malicious Attacks on the Government of National Renewal," proclaimed that the dissemination of "untrue" (that is, critical) statements about the regime was punishable by a term of imprisonment. And although in the very first year of its existence 3744 violations were recorded, Nazi authorities felt the law was not strict enough, and it replaced it one year later with the "Law against Malicious Attacks on the State and the Party and in Defense of Party Uniforms." This new edict included privately made criticisms of the government among the offenses to be punished by incarceration.

The exact wording of the law was as follows:

§1

Whosoever intentionally makes or spreads an untrue or grossly distorted statement of fact of the sort that could seriously damage the welfare of the Empire or the reputation of the Imperial government or the National Socialist German Workers Party is subject, insofar as other statutes do not stipulate a greater punishment, to up to two years' imprisonment. Moreover, if he makes or spreads such a statement in public, he is subject to imprisonment of not less than three months.

Whoever commits such an offense through gross negligence is subject to imprisonment of up to three months or a fine.

If such an offense is directed solely at the reputation of the NSDAP or its members, it will be prosecuted in consultation with the Führer's representative or an officer named by him.

§2

(1) Whosoever makes hostile, incendiary, or belittling public remarks about the leaders of the state or the NS-DAP, or its ordinances or measures, of the sort that could undermine the trust of the people in its political leadership, is subject to imprisonment.

(2) Nonpublic hostile remarks are to be treated as public insofar as the author could or should have reckoned with them becoming public.

(3) Offences will be pursued by order of the Imperial Minister of Justice; if an offence is aimed at a leading personality of the NSDAP, the Imperial Minister of Justice will issue his order in consultation with the Führer's representative.

(4) The Imperial Minister of Justice will determine in consultation with the.Führer's representative which persons are included in the leading personalities of the party in line with paragraph 1.

The law thus accorded the Nazi party and its representatives special legal protection, almost as though they were an endangered species, and also invited Germans to denounce one another.

Even so, the populace was not completely cowed by the new law's harsher terms. It is impossible to determine precisely what effect the changed political climate had upon the telling of political jokes. In the end, the system never functioned as comprehensively as the Nazis would have liked. It wasn't possible to keep all German citizens under surveillance or to watch over what happened in every house and on every street corner. And Germans going about their daily lives no doubt knew that the state was not omnipotent.

Nonetheless, the postwar compilers of Third Reich jokes were convinced that all wisecrackers had lived dangerously. One editor, Kurt Sellin, wrote in the introduction to his book *Hitlerisms in Popular Speech*, published in 1946 with the approval of the Allied occupying forces:

> People often described jokes and irony as being deadly. The Third Reich did not perish because of the jokes that were made about it. And it was not exclusive to the Third Reich that a joke could prove deadly for the person who told it. But the Third Reich did yield a number of instances of precisely that.

Sellin went into great detail about the "personal dangers" that came with telling popular jokes. He also asserts that Germans, fearing draconian punishments, only told political jokes in private, in hushed tones or after first looking around to make sure no one else was listening in. That picture, though, does not conform to the reports of other witnesses interviewed for this book. The majority of them said that they were indeed able to tell political jokes freely, openly, and without fear of punishment.

The historian Meike Wöhlert has analyzed and compared the judgments rendered by courts responsible for malicious acts of treason in five cities. Although her research only deals with registered cases and not unofficial ones, the results suggest that the telling of political jokes was a mass phenomenon beyond state control. In 61 percent of official cases, joke-tellers were let off with a warning, alcohol consumption often being cited as an extenuating circumstance. (People who had had one too many in bars were considered only partially responsible for their actions, and because most of the popular jokes that made it to court had been told in bars, the verdicts were accordingly lenient.) Fines were rarely handed down, and in only 22 percent of cases were those found guilty sentenced to any time in jail. Strangely, the harshest sentences for "maliciousness" were rendered in prewar Nazi Germany, but even then the term of incarceration seldom exceeded five months.

The historical record contradicts the assumption that the Nazis sentenced large numbers of people to death during World War II for telling jokes. In the final phase of the Third Reich, some cases did receive capital sentences, but they were extreme exceptions to the rule. (We will return to them later.) The compilations of jokes that circulated in Germany after the war bore titles like *Deadly Laughter* and *When Laughter Was Dangerous*, but there is not much evidence that the jokes they contained were inevitably risky for the teller.

There is no doubt, however, that the situation became tense after the law was passed enabling the Nazis to legally target their political enemies. Even the adroit Werner Finck had to watch his step. Every night, Nazi "cultural monitors" came to the Catacomb and jotted down everything he said. These spies were so indiscreet that Finck often recognized them and built them into his act. Sometimes, he'd interrupt his performance to address them directly: "Do you want me to talk slower? Are you keeping up? Or should I wait for you?"

The Nazis among Finck's audience weren't amused by these impromptu barbs. In a protocol with the Kafkaesque designation Nr. 41551/35II2C8057/35, the fascist monitors reported the following:

> The Catacomb's audience is largely made up of Jews, who frenetically applaud the common insults and biting, destructive criticism of the performer Werner Fink [sic]. Fink is a typical cultural Bolshevik who apparently does not understand the new times, or in any case doesn't want to, and who tries, in the same manner of earlier Jewish writers, to drag National Socialism and everything holy to National Socialists through the mud.

Two years after Hitler took office, the authorities had had enough and suddenly reversed their policy of ostensible tolerance toward Finck. Up until 1935, the cabaret artist had been given minor roles in state-produced films, such as the harmless comedy *A Fresh Wind from Canada*. But his next role, in the film *April Fools*, was to be his last. Finck was arrested while on the set and taken to the much feared Gestapo headquarters in the center of Berlin.

Finck later recalled that he initially thought the whole thing would be over in an hour. But as the interrogations dragged on, and the time he was scheduled to perform at the Catacomb drew ever nearer, he started to suspect that this time the authorities were serious. What he didn't know was that the premises of his employer had also been closed—forever. After a bit of hemming and hawing, the officials, some of whom were fans of Finck's, told him he was being "kept on." Finck later described the scene, which was not without some black comedy of its own, in his memoirs:

Finally, my watchers had to fess up. In embarrassed and genuinely polite tones, they said they had no other choice but to arrest me. Then they accompanied me to the prison across the way. As I entered, an extremely tall SS man leapt in front of me and asked: "Do you have any weapons?" "Why?" I responded. "Do I need any?"

The Nazi press made a meal of Finck's arrest. The SS organ *Das Schwarze Korps* dismissed the Catacomb as a "cultural refuse heap" and mentioned in passing that other cabaret houses, such as Larifari and the popular Tingel-Tangel, had also been forced to close their doors permanently.

Finck's arrest was part of a larger, concerted action against cabaret performers who had gotten under the Nazis' skin. The measures taken had been planned down to the smallest detail. One of Goebbels's intimates, a Major Trettelsky, had even recommended that the "breeding grounds of Jewish and Marxist propaganda should be closed during their performances and everyone involved, including the audience, should be taken into protective custody."

Not all the performers arrested ended up in jail cells. Ekkehard Arendt pulled out his Nazi Party membership book, for example, and Rudolf Platte expressed regret and swore to change his ways. Both were released. But no such leniency was shown to Finck, Walter Gross, Walter Trautschold, Günter Lüders, or Heinrich Giesen, who were all taken to the Esterwegen concentration camp on Germany's Dutch border. The theater formerly occupied by the Catacomb was taken over by the cabaret troupe Tatzelwurm, whose directors, Tatjana Seis and Bruno Fritz, made sure that any humor in their shows was too harmless to offend the authorities.

For Finck and his colleagues, it was the beginning of a long stretch of hard time. Esterwegen was no extermination camp, but prisoners were hardly treated gently. One form of ordeal there that shouldn't be underestimated was the uncertainty about whether one would ever be released.

Finck was luckier than most inmates: his relative fame and popularity meant he was spared the guards' full brutality. In fact, he was even allowed to stage an evening of cabaret while inside. His routine "Have no fear, we're already here" has been preserved. It's a prime example of Finck's black humor:

> *Comrades, we are going to try to cheer you up, and our sense of humor will help us in this endeavor, although the phrase* gallows humor *has never seemed so logical and appropriate. The external circumstances are exactly in our favor. We need only to take a look at the barbed wire fences, so high and full of electricity. Just like your expectations.*
>
> *And then there are the watchtowers that monitor our every move. The guards have machine guns. But machine guns won't intimidate us, comrades. They just have barrels of guns, whereas we are going to have barrels of laughs.*
>
> *You may be surprised at how upbeat and cheerful we are. Well, comrades, there are goods reasons for this. It's been a long time since we were in Berlin. But every time we appeared there, we felt very uneasy. We were afraid we'd get sent to the concentration camps. Now that fear is gone. We're already here.*

In the end, Finck and his colleagues were imprisoned for only six weeks. This was not due to any mercy on Goebbels' part, but rather to the fact that an actress named Käthe Dorsch who had once been Hermann Göring's lover, intervened on their behalf with him. And Göring was very ready to listen because he loved putting one over on his eternal rival Goebbels. Nonetheless, Finck's release from the concentration camp did not mean the comedian had been pardoned. All the performers from the Catacomb and Tingel-Tangel were required to answer for themselves before a court.

The case was tried in front of the Special Court of the State of Berlin. The defendants were accused of violating the law against "maliciousness," and the proceedings were to go down in cabaret history. The authorities had made the mistake of admitting the public. While prosecutors read out the charges, which consisted almost entirely of political jokes and chanson lyrics, ripples of amusement began to spread among the auditors. The judge then ordered Finck to recapitulate "The Fragment of the Tailor," his most offensive routine from the state's point of view.

The sketch was built around a quick exchange between a tailor and a customer. The tailor asks: "How may I serve you, sir?" To which the customer replies, "Serve, serve—everyone wants to serve! I need leisurewear, warm. There's something chilling in the air." The tailor asks: "For camping?" To which the customer responds, "Camping? No, no—nothing to do with camps!" The tailor then measures the customer's right arm outstretched (the measurements are sly references to the years of communist unrest, 1918–19, and to the year the Nazis seized power, 1933). When the customer doesn't immediately lower his arm, the tailor asks: "Why haven't you put your arm down?" Finally the customer replies: "Right's suspended!"

In front of the court, Finck recited a harmless version of the sketch with garbled punch lines. His coerced performance ended with the words "raised right hand," a reference to the Hitler greeting, and when the prosecutor reminded him that the sketch originally concluded with the phrase "right's suspended," Finck shot back, "You said it, not me." Uproarious laughter broke out in the courtroom. The trial ended with Finck being acquitted for lack of evidence. Finck had survived with just a scare. But he was prohibited from performing for one year, and his employer had fallen victim to the Nazis' cultural cleansing. The courageous wisecracker was a free man once more, but detainment in a concentration camp still represented just the beginning of a caesura in his life.

IN THE END, the Nazis' early pseudo-liberalism and the later intensification of their efforts to eliminate real and imagined political enemies were neither accidents nor creations of the moment. The new, harsher version of Nazism had been a long time coming and indeed had been presaged in 1934 by an outburst of cannibalistic homicide within the party itself. In a party purge that came to be known as the Night of the Long Knives, the SA chief of staff Ernst Röhm and other members of the SA leadership fell victim to this orgy of violence. Once an intimate friend of Hitler's, Röhm had insisted on a "second revolution" as the initial euphoria surrounding Hitler's rise to power began to wane. He wanted more attention paid to the weaker members of German society and also demanded a greater role for the SA.

The ex-soldier saw himself caught between a rock and hard place: the organization he headed was a revolutionary militia that had never had a chance to flex its muscles, thanks to Hitler's nonviolent rise to power. Röhm sought to give the SA more weight in Germany by staging increased numbers of marches and purchasing additional weapons. In doing so, however, he stepped on some powerful toes. He earned the enmity of the Prussian generals in command of the German army by suggesting that Germany's armed forces be subjugated to the SA. At the same time, ordinary Germans feared the SA's uncontrolled thuggery and brutal readiness to turn violent. Röhm and his private army of cloddish thugs, frustrated in their need for action, had few allies, and Röhm's demands and darkly threatening posturing did little to help the SA's reputation.

Hitler had issued a series of warnings aimed at Röhm, voiced first in small circles and then in front of an assembly of the party's district leaders. The gist of these speeches became known to the general populace, who understood the threats they contained. Röhm quickly became the butt of a number of jokes. Significantly, most of the witticisms revolved around Röhm's relatively open homosexuality rather than the violent excesses of his brownshirts.

> *Since Hitler openly complained about the perversions that have taken hold within the SA, people understand what Chief of Staff Röhm really meant when he said, "In every Hitler Youth, there's an SA leader."*

In official Nazi ideology, there was hardly any sin worse than homosexuality. In the male-dominated militarized social order of the new regime, there was no room for "femininity." And a number of stock "gay jokes" were adapted to feature Röhm personally. One example played on the German *Po*, baby talk for "ass," also the name of a river in Italy:

> *Did you hear Röhm is taking his next holiday in Italy? He wants to spent a few days enjoying the warmth of the Po.*

The quips had not been created for Röhm personally; they had already been pointed at similar figures under other governments in German history. They were only political insofar as they were recycled in order to highlight Röhm's fatal weakness for his party comrades.

But Röhm's enemies in 1934 were not content just to draw attention to his violation of mainstream sexual mores. The SA leader's archenemies, above all SS boss Heinrich Himmler and his overambitious deputy Reinhard Heydrich, invented a complicated conspiracy, supposedly headed by Röhm, to topple Hitler's government. On June 30, Hitler struck out with extreme brutality at the alleged "counterrevolutionaries." Accompanied by two armed police detectives, Hitler woke up the leader of the mythical putsch, Röhm, in the middle of the night and had him arrested. Another SA leader and supposed conspirator, Edmund Heines, was dragged out of the bed he was sharing with his male lover.

The arrests were followed by hours of homicidal violence. At least 85 people died in the purge. Röhm was executed on July 2 after he refused to commit suicide. The Night of the Long Knives threw a spotlight on the Nazi regime's true disposition, seen not just in Germany but around the world. And though many cheered the fact that something had finally been done to rein in the louts of the SA, the explosion of bloodshed that had accomplished it was not reassuring. The liquidation of the storm troopers' leadership showed the citizens of Germany that their government would stop at nothing to achieve its ends. A joke soon began to circulate that the German constitution had been changed to read: "The Führer executes the appointment of ministers and, if necessary, the ministers as well."

Hitler himself appeared a bit insecure in the weeks following the assassination of his former ally. In subsequent public speeches, he sometimes justified the killing spree as an act of "state defense" against a planned SA putsch; sometimes he said it had been necessary for moral reasons. On July 13, Hitler addressed the Reichstag with a conspicuously muddled speech. One passage referred directly to Röhm's homosexuality:

> The worst thing was that a sect had begun to form out of a certain common orientation in the SA, which in turn formed the basis of a conspiracy not just against the mores of a healthy people but also against the security of the state.

The German populace gratefully caught the ball that Hitler had unintentionally thrown them and came up with a number of extremely macabre jokes about Röhm's bitter end. Röhm's chauffeur, they cracked, had applied for a widow's pension. And ever since Röhm had gone to heaven, the angels had been wearing their fig leaves on their behinds.

Such jokes made it clear that few tears were shed over the death of the SA chief of staff. But others were potshots at the entire Nazi leadership. One played on Röhm's reputation as a violent revolutionary and a German idiom, *von hinten anfangen*, meaning both "to start from behind" and "to start from the beginning":

> *It's a shame they shot Röhm.*
> *Why?*
> *They say his heart was in the right place. He was about to start over* von hinten.

Another joke, one of the few not to revolve around Röhm's homosexuality, was uncharacteristically blunt about the other Nazi leaders. It played on the double meaning of the word *erhalten* in the phrase *Gott erhalte*, or "God save" (as in "God Save the Queen"), which also means "receive" (as in "God has received Röhm in Heaven"):

> *May God preserve Hitler. May he preserve Göring and Goebbels too. He's already preserved Röhm.*

We do not know how popular this joke was and whether it was told directly after Röhm's assassination or not. But one thing is clear: Germans must have known by that time that their country was in the hands of a terrible regime that didn't shy away from violations of basic human rights, torture, or murder. What should have been apparent with the establishment of the Dachau concentration camp in March 1933 became blindingly obvious after the Night of the Long Knives on July 30, 1934, which claimed not only the lives of the SA leadership but also those of several conservative politicians.

Long after the end of World War II and the demise of the Third Reich, a generation of Germans kept insisting that they knew nothing of the Nazis' crimes. But the jokes popular in the early years when the Nazi regime was still consolidating its power suggest that such claims were untrue, even from the beginning of Hitler's rule.

IV. HUMOR AND PERSECUTION

DURING THE FIRST months of their rule, the Nazis used persecution and murder chiefly to get rid of political opponents, but once they had repressed the Communists, Social Democrats, and bourgeois traditionalists, they quickly turned their sights on German Jews. The more the Nazis consolidated their power, the safer they felt from political opposition, the more destructive force they felt able to direct at this minority, which had previously been solidly integrated into German society. As early as March 1933, marauding SA units had engaged in anti-Semitic violence, although other Nazis were worried about the criticism in the foreign press. Joseph Goebbels and Julius Streicher, the party's leading anti-Semite, wanted to give the go-ahead for a major pogrom on the streets of Germany, but Hitler was more cautious. In the end, the party leadership agreed to call for a national boycott of Jewish-owned shops and Jewish doctors and lawyers. On April 1, armed SA men took up positions in front of Jewish businesses and tried to prevent customers from spending money in them. Some troops painted anti-Semitic slogans and Stars of David on display windows; others were content to hold up signs calling for a boycott and to curse at Jewish businessmen. Some areas also saw looting and acts of violence.

All in all, this display of activism made a very negative impression on most people, and the thuggish SA men with their uneducated bellowing were left even less popular among the general population than they had been before. Although very few

Germans openly declared their solidarity with their Jewish fellow citizens, the boycott did not, as it was intended to do, set German gentiles against German Jews. On the contrary, ordinary people felt sorry for them, and if reports by the Nazis, who were disappointed by the boycott, are to be believed, the amount of commerce done afterward by Jewish-owned business did not decline at all.

Jewish Germans came up with a number of jokes revolving around the boycott, the first nationwide anti-Semitic initiative carried out by the Nazi government. One running theme—hardly a surprise—was the arbitrary nature of this state coercion. Despite the considerable horror they had felt when the SA men were bellowing crude anti-Semitic slogans, in retrospect the joke-tellers were very much aware of the boycott's inherent absurdity:

> *A city on the Rhine during the boycott: SA men stand in front of Jewish businesses and "warn" passers-by against entering them. Nonetheless, a woman tries to go into a knitting shop.*
>
> *An SA man stops her and says, "Hey, you. Stay outside. That's a Jewish shop!"*
>
> *"So?" replies the woman. "I'm Jewish myself."*
>
> *The SA man pushes her back. "Anyone can say that!"*

The punch line played on the fact that it was usually impossible to tell the difference between gentile and Jewish Germans.

The boycott made it clear that the Nazis were serious about their promise to drive even fully assimilated Jews out of German society. Germany's relatively small Jewish minority was made into a magnet for racist resentments that were deeply anchored in the German social core. In the copious propaganda that accompanied the boycott, Jews were made the scapegoats, however improbably, for a whole range of social ills, though in many rural regions of Germany there were no Jews at all—a fact that give rise to the following joke:

> *Julius Streicher, the spokesman for the anti-Jewish boycott, received a telegram from a small town in northern Germany. It read: "Send Jews immediately—stop—otherwise boycott impossible."*

The boycott was the first of what soon seemed an endless series of anti-Jewish measures, minutely described in the diaries of Viktor Klemperer and other chroniclers of the time. The Third Reich did not begin with Auschwitz. The extermination camps were the terrible culmination reached after German anti-Semitism had been ratcheted up over several years. The earliest anti-Semitic laws were aimed at forcing as many Jews as possible to emigrate, since the state was eager to get its hands on the property that would be left behind by those who—in Nazi terminology—"pulled out."

The inaugural piece of official anti-Semitic legislation by the Nazi government was the "Law for the Restoration of the Professional Civil Service," enacted April 7, 1935. This law sent all "non-Aryan civil servants" into forced early retirement and arbitrarily defined non-Aryans to be those persons with at least one Jewish grandparent. A certificate of heritage was introduced, and the stricture on civil servants was later extended to notary publics, midwives, druggists, and other professionals. This absurd piece of official paper was also required to obtain a loan and even made a qualification for a certificate of sports training.

Those Jews who remained in Germany relieved their frustration with gallows humor:

"What is the most desirable woman?"—"An Aryan grand-mother, of course."—"No, that's wrong."—"So who is it then?"—"A Jewish great-grandmother. She brought money into the family but not any trouble!"

Another early legislative low point was the "Law for the Protection of German Blood and German Matrimony," which prohibited gentile-Jewish marriages and extramarital sexual relationships. Violations of this law were liable to draconian punishments. According to a somewhat clumsy pun at the time, there was no need to worry about "race shame" (the Nazi term for intermarriage) any more. The reason, according to the joke, was that rich Jews had all moved abroad, leaving only the poor ones behind, and there was no shame in poverty.

AROUND THE SAME time that the German judiciary decided to intrude into all citizens' sex lives, Jewish Germans were subjected to a never-ending battery of other prohibitions. They were no longer allowed to employ "Aryan" servants, drive cars, fly German flags, or send their children to school. Jewish joke-tellers trained a tragicomic eye on many of these senseless restrictions:

A school inspector visits a classroom and sees a blond girl sitting all alone on a bench. The inspector takes pity on her and asks, "Why are sitting all by yourself, my child?" The girl answers, "Ask Grandma."

A Jewish child forced to listen to his teacher's anti-Semitic tirades in school goes home and asks his parents, "Mama, Papa, can't you exchange me for some other kid?"

Some sectors of the German population may have felt for their Jewish countrymen, and a few may have gotten involved on their behalf. But the vast majority of people watched the daily harassments in silence, and some joined in wherever possible.

The following anecdote makes it clear just how much Jewish Germans had to endure in the run-up to World War II:

An elegant old lady is unable to find anywhere to sit on a streetcar. No matter where she looks there's no gentleman willing to stand up. A modest young Jewish girl offers to rise, but the lady recoils in horror at a "Jewish" seat. At that point, an older gentleman stands up gravely and points out that his seat is pure "Aryan."

Seldom did Germans lift a finger to defend their Jewish fellow citizens. On the contrary, many were eager to take over jobs vacated by Jews who were fired or forced to emigrate. On September 30, 1933, for example, when thousands of Jewish attorneys lost their right to practice, their "Aryan" colleagues were only too glad to inherit their clients and cases.

One joke from the time reflected this situation, playing on the dual meaning of the word *Klage*: "complaint" and "lawsuit." One man asks another, "How are you doing," and the response is: "Like a Jewish lawyer: no complaints."

The rigor with which Jews were persecuted increased with each passing year. Jews were banned from using park benches, visiting cinemas, and even keeping house pets. Many Jews now recognized the turn things were taking and fled into exile. The property they left behind was auctioned off to grateful Aryans at bargain-basement prices and without any compensation paid to the owners. Germans, always hungry for a good deal, thronged to such auctions.

The Jews who remained in Germany, however, risked losing not only their belongings, but also their lives. Yet many of them continued to make light of their increasingly precarious position:

Levi and Hirsch bump into one another in the wilderness of Sudan. Each of them is carrying a heavy rifle and leading a column of bearers. "How it going," asks one. "What are you doing here?" "I've got an ivory-carving shop in Alexandria, and to keep costs down, I shoot the elephants myself. And you?" "Much the same. I've got a crocodile leather business in Port Said and am here hunting for crocs." "And what's the story with our friend Simon?" "Oh, he's a real adventurer. He stayed in Berlin."

But life was hardly a walk in the park for Jewish émigrés, either, since they were seldom welcomed with open arms abroad. During the first great Jewish-German exodus, many intellectual Jews went to Austria, but despite the common language, few managed to establish themselves in the smaller, alpine nation. Austrian unemployment in the 1930s reached catastrophic levels. According to some estimates more than half a million people were out of work, and those in search of day labor could be found waiting on every street corner. The Austrian government, led by the anti-Nazi but fascist Engelbert Dollfuss, completely failed in its attempts to bring the economy under control. Jewish-German cabaret artists and comedians had it even harder than other émigré job-seekers, since Austria already had an established Jewish cabaret scene, led by Fritz Grünbaum, Karl Farkas, and Jura Soyfer. Those newcomers lucky enough to get an engagement often played to empty houses.

In short, many of these early refugees were forcing their way into a country that was already in desolate shape. Dollfuss was assassinated in 1934, and his successor, Kurt Schuschnigg, was spineless and unpopular. With the support of the German government, Austrian Nazis constantly tried to pour oil on these social flames, staging a series of garish propaganda events and engaging in an ever increasing number of anti-Semitic outrages. The situation was poisonous, but nonetheless, Austria remained the chosen destination for most Jewish-German émigrés of the early 1930s.

The popular character actor Kurt Gerron was one of those who sought refuge on the banks of the Danube. He moved there in 1934, six years after playing the street singer in "Mack the Knife" at the triumphant world premier of Brecht's *Threepenny Opera* in Berlin. He had also acted alongside Marlene Dietrich in the film *The Blue Angel* and begun a successful career as a director of cinema comedies. Then, suddenly, he was on the outside looking in. On April 1, 1933, the day of the boycott, the production director had come on the set where Gerron was making a film and announced, "Those who don't have pure Aryan blood must leave the studio immediately." Magda Schneider, who played the female lead in the film, later recalled that the hulking Gerron went terribly pale and left the set with hunched shoulders. None of the other participants made any effort to defend him.

Otto Wallburg, Gerron's colleague, the Jewish comedian who was known for his blubbering manner of speech, was allowed to stay on in German films because he promptly applied for a "temporary" work permit. There was still no law forbidding Jewish actors from practicing their trade, but protesting against company decisions was fruitless. Those complaints that were filed were summarily rejected. Gerron, recognizing the hopelessness of his situation in the new Nazi empire, decided not to take his former employer to court, and to leave Germany. "If things turn out okay here," he remarked to Wallburg, "my name is Moritz." Responsibility for the film he was directing was handed over to the Nazi loyalist Hans Steinhoff. Steinhoff's star was to rise in the Third Reich, and he later directed one of the most popular Nazi films, *Hitler Youth Quex*. Gerron, in contrast, stood on the brink of a decade of abysmal suffering that would end in his death.

When he arrived in the overcrowded, politically explosive Austrian capital, Gerron pulled off a rare coup, for an émigré, by immediately landing a job. For Tobis Studios, he directed a romantic comedy entitled *Boards that Mean the World*. It starred Wallburg, who had followed Gerron into exile. But despite a famous cast, the film was a financial flop. Movies made by Jews could not be sold in Germany, and the Austrian market was too small to cover costs. Before long, Viennese studio bosses avoided Gerron and cut off his cash flow.

In the meantime, Gerron's parents and wife had joined him in Austria, and that made his financial situation even more complicated, so after eighteen months, he decided to move on. Initially he went to The Hague in Holland, a country that took in émigrés with open arms. Jewish performers who chose to stay in Vienna were in for a rude awakening. Before long, Hitler began casting a greedy eye on the country of his birth.

The other Alpine nation, Switzerland, would remain a safe haven for the duration of the Third Reich—for those Jews who managed to get in. Swiss immigration policies were tough, and the country's relationship with Nazi Germany was ambivalent. The Swiss government never took a clear stand against the inhuman practices of its much larger neighbor. Swiss official attitudes ranged from diplomatic caution to callous indifference when it came to the suffering of would-be émigrés. And against this background of official silence, the Swiss fascist movement became ever more vocal in its demands for political authority.

Pro-Nazi fascists in Zürich took especial umbrage at the political cabaret house Cornichon, and Walter Lesch, the founder of this cultural institution, became enemy number one for those on the far right. All of the issues on which the Swiss government chose to remain silent were paraded in front of a paying audience night after night in Lesch's theater. The satire was so cutting that on numerous occasions Germany's Foreign Minister von Ribbentrop filed official complaints with the Swiss government. But neither those complaints nor the whining of Swiss fascists had any effect. Despite calls for the theater to be censored or closed, Cornichon's doors remained open.

The theater became a magnet for the German cabaret scene in exile, a venue where performers could heap scorn and ridicule on the Nazis without fear of retribution. Lesch himself ratcheted up the atmosphere with anti-German songs featuring lyrics far more uncompromising than to be found anywhere else in the Alpine countries. In 1938, he composed this song, with rhyming lyrics in the original, about a nation called Nazidonia and its favorite enemy: `

"He's to Blame for It All"

In Nazidonia, happy land
Where the original Aryans throng,
Reich of a thousand little years
And the racially pure marriage-band
Comes a leader, big and strong,
Promising butter, blood, and cream.
Yet though he like a Wotan stand

Bellowing out his glorious songs
Ruling the land at the top of his lungs,
Cooking fat's still an impossible dream.
And the Führer keeps a sharp eye out
For the insidious assassin
Since it stands beyond a doubt
That someone's to blame for the mess we're in.
And lo and behold, look at that.
The villain's already been found,
Isidore, ever degenerate,
Is guilty of this too, the hound!
And to punish his malice, vile and depraved,
He's stripped of money and passport for that,
And though they still have no cooking fat,
The people think they have been saved.

And the moral of the story
To make it short and sweet
If it weren't for the evil Jew
How could we rule the state?

In Italy, in Italy
The land of musicality
Hateful crows now call their song
From the roofs of palaces,
The lira barely limps along,
And Il Duce's terribly concerned,
That in far Abyssinia
Where the palms and pine trees sway
No one can rule as he please
Or stroll the sands unburned.

But the leader cannot err, and thus
There's no possible conclusion
But that known traitors, foes to us,
O'er the Po spread their confusion
Just as everywhere they do.
And the culprit we already know.
Signor Cohen, so it seems,
And his usual traitor's schemes.
If someone breaks his neck in two,
The people, though they still get fleeced,
Think their suffering is eased.

And the moral of the case
Remains the same in every place:
If it weren't for the evil Jew,
What would scapegoat-seekers do?

In Romania, Romania
(Yes, why not in Romania?)
Even the little children there
Have to have their evil Jew.
How else could their rulers dare
To hoodwink them the way they do?
They had to do whatever they could
To pull the wool over their eyes
They'll always need a good scapegoat
To smear with muddy lies.
German, Roman, and Japanese,
Fresh and chaste, and Franco-Spanish,
One can only destroy a people's right
By giving them something to execute,

Communist or evil Jew,
But Bible scholar or Catholic, too,
Any one of them will do
To keep us from hating the ones we should.
But soon as all the scapegoats vanish
We're the ones whose throats get slit
And the people are victims of the crime,
And still they simply don't get it.

And the moral of the rhyme
Until the very end of time?
If there were no evil Jew
We would miss him, me and you.

Another Zürich cabaret house, Pfeffermühle ("Pepper Mill") was somewhat more discreet, packaging political criticism in allusion and metaphors. This troupe was formed in 1933 by Klaus and Erika Mann, the children of Thomas Mann. Klaus Mann later described the project as "a literary cabaret with a strong political focus and a playful but deeply serious and impassioned protest against the shame of fascism." He added: "The texts for most of the numbers—chansons, recitations, sketches—were by Erika, although I wrote some. Erika was the emcee, director, and main organizer. She sang, whipped up enthusiasm, hired the employees, inspired the performers—and in short she was the heart and soul of the whole theater."

The original Pfeffermühle had been in Munich, but the audience there was full of Nazi spies, and the fascist press waged a constant campaign to stir up public animosity against the small house. After the Reichstag fire, the political atmosphere became too dangerous for left-wing cabaret. But the troupe found that even in

Switzerland political humor was a risky enterprise, and most of the Swiss public were turned off by satire disguised as allegory.

A good example of the Pfeffermühle's style is the following text by Erika Mann, which was transparently about Hitler:

I am the prince of the land of lies
I can lie to shake the trees
Good lord, am I a skillful liar!
No one lies so brilliantly.

I lie so inventively
That the blue falls from the sky
See lies flying through the air
That lying gale's source am I.

Now summer is a-comin' in
And the trees are all in bud
The field are full of violets
And war does not shed blood.

Ha, ha. You fell for it.
In your faces I can read it.
Although it was completely false,
Every one of you believed it.

Lying is nice
Lying is fine
Lying brings luck
Lying bucks you up.
Lying has lovely long legs.

Lies make you rich
Lies are well-stitched
Seem like they're true
Wash sin from you
And follow on a leash like dogs.

Back in my home, the land of lies,
The truth must remain unspoken.
A colorful web of lying strands
Keeps our great Empire unbroken.

We have it good, we have it nice
We kill all our enemies
And award ourselves the highest device
Of honor for our false glories.

Once a liar, nevermore trusted;
Always a liar, always believed!
That he speaks anything but truth
Is an utterly intolerable idea.

Lying is easy
Everything's grand
If you can do it,
False means to our end.
To the land of lies
Lying brings fame
Lies are colorful and elegant
While gray truth looks always the same.

In order to protect my land

I mix the poison and set the fires
If you doubt me, I'll shut you up,
I, the prince of the land of lies.

By 1934 the fascist Swiss National Front was staging violent protests inside the theater. Glasses and chairs were thrown, while the fascists chanted "Jews get out" and "We don't need Jews in Switzerland." Instead of receiving help from Swiss authorities, the Manns had to publicly defend their political project. Before long, representatives of the Third Reich began flexing their muscles at the Swiss government, which responded by passing a law forbidding foreign residents of Switzerland from making political statements. Appeasement was the policy of choice in Europe, and Germany's smaller neighbors hoped that compromise would pacify Hitler.

When Switzerland's political leaders caved to Nazi bullying, it was the end for Klaus and Erika Mann's cabaret. In response to the new law, Erika Mann sent an open letter to the most influential Swiss newspaper, justifying her work:

The Pfeffermühle is not a stage for inciting the masses or promoting a political party, nor is it an émigré theater. It's an association of young people of various nationalities (Swiss, German, Russian, Austrian) who are trying to offer respectable entertainment and amuse people in a way that makes them think. "The Pfeffermühle would like you to think about..." could be the slogan on our programs and invitations. We are trying, in a consciously light-hearted manner, to say serious things that need to be said today. And we'd have every reason to be ashamed, if we stopped doing that now.

In 1937, after the Manns had emigrated to the United States, Erika and Klaus made a brief attempt at reviving their theater in New York, but people there weren't particularly interested in either cabaret or the problems of continental Europeans. Despite its ultimate demise, however, the Pfeffermühle was certainly the most successful and influential émigré cabaret troupe of the period.

Its fate was symptomatic of the situation faced by politically active exiles in the years prior to World War II. Many host countries issued gag orders, but the status of political refugees in Switzerland was particularly precarious. The Swiss were quite xenophobic and constantly feared being overrun by foreigners. Because she was married to the poet W.H. Auden, who carried a British passport, Erika Mann was not affected by the country's strict visa regulations. But for Jewish émigrés, whom Switzerland did not acknowledge as political refugees, a German-Swiss border crossing was too often merely a detour on the way to the concentration camp. "Escort out" was what the Swiss called the deportations, and in many cases it was an escort to the grave.

THE SITUATION of Jews in Germany was getting worse and worse. Jews were constantly being hassled in a variety of ways, and the public insults and government-supported attacks were augmented by the hateful scorn meted out by newspapers like *Der Stürmer*, the organ of Julius Streicher, which published caricatures of Jews that could hardly have been more primitive, and plastered its front pages with every sort of anti-Semitic cliché.

The paper was conspicuously and perhaps revealingly obsessed with the idea that Jews wanted to sexually defile young Aryan women. The repressed pornography and homoeroticism of the illustrations that accompanied articles on this topic were also a grotesque reflection of the era's fascination with physiognomy. The crooked nose, *Der Stürmer* proclaimed, was the most significant and prominent external sign of Jewishness. Lascivious Jewish "race defilers" were depicted with hair slicked back in the manner of Latin lovers; Jewish bankers, who supposedly lusted for Aryans' money, were caricatured as repulsively obese creatures with shifty eyes. One such figure was shown trying to break open strongboxes; another was depicted squatting atop a globe and shitting on it. The world as seen in the *Der Stürmer* was full of perversion, and the sick minds that conceived it were ruling Germany on behalf of the German people.

Above all, those Nazi cartoons were frighteningly perfect visual mirror images of the worldview of the supreme Nazi leader, one he had laid out himself, in *Mein Kampf*:

> The black-haired Jewish youth loiters around for hours, with Satanic glee on his face, for an innocent girl whose blood he defiles and thus takes away from her own people.

The letters to the editor published in *Der Stürmer* were full of similar expressions of adolescent sexual envy. The same was true of the anti-Semitic humor they contributed. Another popular theme was Jewish rapacity and greed, and *Der Stürmer*'s readership came up with endless variations on it in the jokes they invented:

> *Pinkus and a Gentile are attacked in the forest, and as the highwaymen are about to frisk them, Pinkus takes out his wallet and says to his fellow victim: "Ah, I just remembered. I owe you 500 schillings."*

Jokes of this sort were in constant circulation and reinforced and confirmed popular anti-Jewish stereotypes. And though the readership of the *Stürmer* may have collected and passed them on, anti-Jewish jokes were also told by apolitical Germans. They were a symptom of the latent anti-Semitism that had survived beneath the surface of German society and long before the Nazis took power had laid the groundwork for the persecution of Jews in the Third Reich. The line between harmless kidding and defamatory jokes full of resentment was blurry, and not every joke-teller may have been aware of when he crossed the border from mere bad taste to injuriousness.

Nonetheless, even naively repeated clichés helped ostracize the once completely integrated Jewish minority. Once Jews were seen by the public as outsiders or intruders, the authorities could do with them what they wanted. In this sense, no anti-Jewish joke, however mild, was harmless. Moreover, making light of Jews against the backdrop of their persecution, disappropriation, and forced exile was heartless and cyclical, and it gave a gloss of legitimacy to those acts of injustice. The difference between Nazi-era jokes about money-mad Jews and the jokes about tightwad Scotsmen that were popular after the war (many of the latter were adaptations of the former), was that the Scots were not a persecuted minority in Germany, nor was there widespread resentment against them.

Jews were not only moneygrubbers, according to Nazi wits, they were also Communists—another anti-Semitic cliché. The following joke, recorded by a housewife in Westphalia, was very popular. It was probably invented by a Nazi newspaper editor:

Trotsky, Lenin, and Litvinov are walking through a small Russian town, and the children on the street shout, "We

know who you are, we know who you are." Trotsky turns
proudly to his companions and says, "You see how famous
we are. Even kids recognize us." Whereupon the children
run away, shouting, "You're Jews, you're Jews."

Maxim Litvinov, the Soviet Foreign Minister, like Trotsky, did have a Jewish background, and that made him a favorite target for anti-Semitic propagandists; the Nazi press referred to him as "the Jew Finkelstein." To the Nazis, Litvinov embodied everything that was wrong with the world and was living proof of the intrinsic connection between Bolshevism and Jewishness. In Germany, he was seen not as a human being but as a grotesque two-dimensional parody of one—an evil cartoon.

There were even jokes that laughed at anti-Jewish violence, and these were told not just by hardcore Nazi party supporters, but also by hordes of willing opportunists and March violets. According to one example, recorded in a variety of sources, the word RADIO stood for "Rein Arischer Darf Itzig Ohrfeigen"—"a pure Aryan is allowed to box Isaac's ears." Fervent Nazis by no means had a monopoly on this kind of tasteless cynicism. The violent fantasies of most Nazis were shared by many "nonpolitical" Germans. The constant stream of anti-Semitic propaganda likely contributed to this, but ordinary Germans seemed to have come up with the majority of anti-Jewish jokes on their own—a troubling indication of a fundamental animosity toward Jews and Jewishness.

By no means was humor in Nazi Germany confined to "whispered jokes" critical of the regime. The majority of jokes about contemporary affairs were entirely harmless and without any political message. But there was also a plethora of jokes colored by National Socialist ideology, although after World War II nobody wanted to remember those. In contrast, judging by the recollections of those who were there, popular humor that was openly critical of the government was relatively rare.

Some of these more daring political jokes did survive, however, though many can be understood only by reconstructing their original historical context. One topic that particularly inspired the German imagination was the country's withdrawal from the League of Nations, one of Hitler's early "coups" in the realm of foreign policy. The Weimar government had fought hard for years for German membership in the League, but now German nationalists believed that the long-drawn-out disarmament negotiations in Geneva had brought their country nothing but disadvantages. Many Germans still felt a sense of shame over their defeat in World War I and saw the victorious nations' demands for reparation as draconian. The Nazi government was especially outraged that the victors wanted to impose a kind of parole on them: France, in particular, demanded that Germany should only be allowed to raise an army comparable to those of other European powers after a four-year period of good behavior. Hitler, who derided the League as little more than a debating club, responded by provoking a diplomatic spat and withdrawing his representatives.

He then confirmed the legitimacy of this surprising move by holding a plebiscite. The Nazis won the vote by an overwhelming margin. It was effectively the end of the League.

Hardly anyone in Germany shed a tear over the demise of an organization they saw as an instrument of German subordination. The following joke makes that abundantly clear:

During a meeting of the League of Nations in Geneva, a package was delivered containing the note: "For distribution and use." The package was full of nooses.

Another joke began with the idea that a restaurant was serving a new League of Nations cheese. When asked what that was, the waiter responded: "a cheese that melts away on its own."

The jokes about the League of Nations were a mixture of defiance and megalomania. Completely frustrated by the Geneva negotiations, Germans had greeted Hitler's childish gesture as a liberating blow. They liked the notion, propagated by their Führer, that withdrawal from the League was a sign of their renewed vigor and independence. And when Germany commenced its massive rearmament program, which violated a host of international agreements, new jokes arose, full of nationalist boasting:

What does it mean when the sky is black? So many planes are in the air that the birds have to take to the ground.

Later, in the early phase of World War II, when Nazi Germany enjoyed success, the wags in the street made fun of the country's defeated enemies: "The Pope has arrived in Warsaw. He's giving Poland extreme unction."

The humor of the Third Reich was that of the victor and reflected the arrogance that comes from the belief that one has been proven right. The feelings of inferiority that had accrued during the Weimar period disappeared in the intoxication of Nazi military triumph. Humility was off the agenda, as more and more Germans began putting on superhuman airs and looking down with contempt at their supposed inferiors. Popular jokes celebrated the leaders of an empire that was supposed to last a thousand years and heaped scorn upon the vanquished:

Who is Germanys greatest electrician? Adolf Hitler. He

connected Austria, cut off Russia, electrified the entire world, and is still the one flicking the switches.

A similar gag, about German photography, had Hitler pressing the button and Mussolini doing the developing—and as for deposed Czech president Edvard Benes, well, the German word for making photographic prints was also a slang term for turning one's tail.

The humor of many professional joke-tellers was equally supercilious. A moderator of a TV program for Nazi state television (which never got beyond the experimental stage) was filmed threatening critics in a series of puns about internment in concentration camps. There's no record today, so we'll never know whether the following routine, which was performed with a grin, actually made the studio audience laugh:

> *Let's return to the topic of music. I'm glad almost all of us are playing to the same rhythm. And even if there are some queer pipers whistling out of tune or beating a different drum, it's no big deal. They'll be given some further instruction in a "concertation camp" until they've learned their do-re-mi's and accustomed themselves to keeping proper time.*

Hitler and his cohorts liked the idea of using cabaret routines to threaten dissidents. The pompous dictator who loved to pose publicly as an emperor also had his lighter side: he enjoyed popular entertainment and crude jokes. Hitler was reputedly often consumed by laughter at the bon mots of his friend and photographer Heinrich Hoffmann, whom he repeatedly invited to share evenings of jokes with himself and Goebbels. The Nazi leadership who ruthlessly turned their goons on Jewish comedians and opposition cabaret performers were not at all immune to humor, as long as it toed the party line.

Even the ever suspicious Minister of Propaganda had nothing against a performer like Rudi Godden making fun of degenerate modern art in the fascist cabaret troupe *Die acht Entfesselten*. Nor was there any need for Nazi spies to monitor Tatzelwurm, the troupe that took over the space previously used by the banned Catacomb. Hitler and Goebbels made frequent public appearances in Germany's temples of light entertainment; variety theaters were allowed to stay open even in the final phase of World War II; and popular performers were exempted from military service, thanks to a "Führer's list" personally drawn up by Hitler. For the amusement of Germany's leader, Goebbels staged private galas that featured comely dancing girls and Nazi comedians. Hitler and his entourage often stayed up until the wee hours of the morning laughing at the conformist jokes of stylish cabaret performers like Jupp Hussels and Manfred Lommel.

In the weekly newsreels, the Nazi leaders of course went back to behaving like the serious movers and shakers of the world they fancied themselves to be. The only occasions on which Hitler displayed his individual sense of humor, which was based on insults, were his attempts to make his enemies laughable. He called British Prime Minister Neville Chamberlain the "umbrella fella," Roosevelt a "cripple," Churchill a "drunk," and Duff Cooper, Britain's minister of war, a Bavarian dialect term that translates roughly as "inflated chicken."

The cover of Putzi Hanfstaengel's 1933 book *Hitler in World Caricature*.

In Hanfstaengel's book, the caricatures were all
accompanied by "corrective" glosses.

Adolf

*Der Häuptling vom Stamm der wilden Kopfjäger nach der
Schlacht von Leipzig — in vollem Kriegsschmuck*

The caption reads: The chief of a tribe of wild headhunters in
full war dress after the Battle of Leipzig.

A caricature by E. O. Plauen

Fritz Peter taught his chimpanzee to do the Hitler salute.

Werner Finck, around 1935

The cast of the Catacomb

Weiß Ferdl.

Karl Valentin.

Willi Schaeffer's Cabaret of Comedians

A 1933 Pfeffermühle program.

Fritz Grünbaum (left) and Oskar Sima in
A Song, A Kiss, A Girl from 1932.

Kurt Gerron, 1927.

Etwas zum Lachen

Erst das Geschäft

Levysohn, Pinkus und Marcus wollten sich taufen
...en. Levysohn betritt als erster das Pfarrhaus. Außen
...ten die anderen schon eine halbe Stunde. Levy-
...am nicht zurück. Endlich streckt er grinsend
...e Fratze aus der Türe.
"Nu?!", schreien die beiden anderen. "Biste end-
...e Goi!"
"Mir haben noch garnich gefangen an", erklärt
...sohn, "hab ihm zuerst verkauft en
...hbbzauger!"

Erinnerung an die Inflation

Es war im heurigen Sommer. Isidor und Abraham
...schreiten zur Badeanstalt. An der Kasse mußten sie
...zenig Eintritt bezahlen.
"Gott, wie billig", staunte Isidor. "Wie ich ge-
...ch habe das letzte Mal, mußte ich be-
...len tausend Mark."

Er zahlt drauf

...d blau ist sehr traurig:
Seit 3 Jahren zahle ich ununterbrochen auf mein
...hl drauf!"
...gt ein anderer:
"...o, warum sperren Sie denn dann nicht zu?"
...a ist empört:
"...ber Gott, wovon soll ich dann leben?"

Das Darlehen

...Pinkus und ein Nichtjude sind im Walde von
...erfallen worden. Eben schicken sich die

Wegelagerer an, die beiden auszuplündern. Da zieht
Pinkus schnell seine Brieftasche heraus und sagt zu
seinem Leidensgenossen:
"Ja, richtig, ich bin Ihnen noch 500 Schilling
schuldig, da haben Sie sie zurück!"

In der Straßenbahn

Levy und Moses unterhalten sich.
"Gestern hat mich der Schaffner in der Straßen-
bahn angeschaut, wie wenn ich noch nicht bezahlt
hätte."
"Und was hast du da gemacht?"
"Ich habe ihn zurückangeschaut, wie wenn ich
doch bezahlt gehabt hätte!"

Kleine Nachrichten

Was das Volk nicht verstehen kann

Der Milchkontrolleur Andreas Mändle in Zinzler unterhält
Beziehungen zu den in Turbach noch ansässigen Juden. Am
19. März 1939, mittags 12.30 Uhr unterhielt er sich freundschaft-
lich mit der Seßjudin Else Strauß.

Der Mengermeister Josef Be...
(Rheinland) beschmierte am 17. Ju...
der Hermann-Göring-Straße den...
mit den Worten: "Na, Philipp,...
Daraufhin betrat der Jude be...

Der Obermeister Anton Gü...
der Jude Salomon aus Neust...

Der Kohlenhändler und Jude...
Schwabe, wohnhaft in der Montag...
beschwerte am 26. Juni 1939...
Jsrael Sternberg aus der Kontra...
horn, wobei der Jude neben ihm a...

Im Marienarien-Katalog Nr...
Karl May Deppe in der Einweih...

Der St. Karl Dorlmutter, wo...
...n Bauern, grüßte am 9. Juli De...

Etwas zum Lachen

La Fontaine, Wasserkraft und Binfeld

In dem in Elsaß-Lothringen erscheinenden Kampfblatt
"Das Volk" ist folgende Geschichte veröffentlicht:

Lieber Stürmer!

Auf einem Boulevard in Paris sehen drei von
unserem Volk beisammen, der Ophthalmologe Bärmann, der Kron-Städteder und der Raphael
Hirschbrand, sagen über die schönsten Prei-
sen, wie oft ihr so schwer zu machen einen riesigen
Reibel, wie sich schon ganz mild in der Hand von
vielen Reben.

Geht einer vorbei, der schön richtig gekleidet ist und
Pariser Art. "Na", sagt der Bärmann, "sieh der
La Fontaine Holz in der letzten Zeit." "Bild er
gewesen weismaser", sagt der Städteder, "das
ich was getan ist in Berlin, bei er gedachte
WasserkBraht." "Gott der Gerechter", sagt der
Raphael Hirschbrand, "daß ich so es getan in
Krakau, bei es gedachte Binfeld."

A Stürmer caricature.

Kurt Gerron in the Theresienstadt concentration camp, Fall 1944.

HITLER'S BIZARRE sense of humor displayed his utter inability to make fine distinctions, and he wasn't the only one in Nazi Germany who suffered from this deficiency. Even professional film comedians told terrible jokes. One of the fascists' favorite entertainers was Munich singer and actor Weiß Ferdl, who had been in close contact with the Nazi leadership since the 1920s. In the Third Reich he became a huge star. Besides recording Reich-friendly songs, the Bavarian performer acted in a series of supremely shallow comedies. The idiotic highpoint was the 1939 film *The Laughing Doctor*, in which Ferdl, playing a country physician, mugged his way through a simpleminded plot. This thigh-slapping humor was gussied up with blondes in dirndls and a supporting cast who looked like the product of centuries of Alpine incest. The conformist German press sang their praises of this example of Bavarian pseudo-comedy, choosing Ferdl as their particular darling. That, combined with the Führer's own enthusiasm for it, meant a quantum leap in the singer's career. Hitler arranged a private screening of *The Laughing Doctor* at his Obersalzberg mountain retreat.

Comedian Karl Valentin was infinitely more talented than Ferdl, but he did not enjoy the dubious favor of the ruling elite, who considered his subtle, anarchic folk humor at odds with mainstream Nazi values. Valentin also had a reputation as a left-winger, although he refrained from making political statements and sent the Cultural Chamber a letter disavowing critical jokes that had been attributed to him. But his protestations got him nowhere. In 1936, his completely apolitical film *The Inheritance* was banned for "sordid tendencies." Karl Valentin and Liesl Karstadt, his partner from many a slapstick classic, were forbidden to work. It was an ignominious, unworthy end for the best comedy duo Germany ever had. Valentin, the leading light of German humor on film, today considered Germany's Charlie Chaplin, withdrew deeply embittered from the public eye.

IN PLACE OF the clever slapstick they had banned, Goebbels and his minions filled German cinemas with lowest-common-denominator fascist "comedies" produced by directorial dilettantes such as Carl Froelich and Wolfgang Liebeneiner. Card-carrying Nazi Party members who demonstrated loyalty in public were able to go far in the glitzy world of the state-run UFA film studios, no matter how slim their talent. The jobs vacated by Jewish artists driven into exile had to be filled by someone. The rigorous political purges in Germany's entertainment industry gave rise to some absurd situations. In 1934, audiences were still enjoying films and hit songs made by Jewish artists whom movie moguls had already been forced to emigrate. Film companies, which were still largely in private hands, defended their schizophrenic policies by saying they couldn't afford to simply throw away all films in which Jews had participated.

By 1935, however, German cinema had been thoroughly Nazified, and movies with Jewish actors disappeared from theaters. The Imperial Chamber of Culture took care that German actors who were considered politically unreliable, like Werner Finck and Karl Valentin, got no work, and state film subsidies were subject to tight control. If a producer made himself unpopular with the Nazi elite, the latter simply turned off the money. By the end of the 1930s, most of the film industry had been nationalized, and all scripts under consideration had to be submitted to the notoriously suspicious Goebbels. Proactive censorship allowed the Propaganda Minister to get filmmakers on board with the party line before they started production. Naturally, the results of such a system were abysmally stupid.

Ninety percent of all films made during the Third Reich were insignificant, superficial comedies intended to distract Germans from state terrorism and, later, the hardships of war. They seemed to be completely apolitical: audiences seldom saw even a Nazi salute or a swastika flag; the realities of life under the Reich were systematically filtered out. The storylines featured the stock twists and turns of romantic comedy, and the Aryan casts went through the prescribed motions until the inevitable happy ending. It's difficult to imagine today how people could have found this sort of state-controlled kitsch amusing. Yet German moviegoers seemed to enjoy them, and few noticed that in fact they were subtly laced with propagandistic messages.

A GOOD EXAMPLE is the work of Heinz Rühmann, who was also one of the most popular singers and actors after Hitler's defeat. His film *Quax, the Crash-Happy Pilot*, which suggested that flyboys in the German air force led a pretty jolly life, came out when the Luftwaffe desperately needed human material on the Eastern Front. And the Rühmann vehicle *Hooray, I'm a Father* was made because Goebbels wanted to motivate Germans to have more children. "The Führer needs soldiers," Goebbels remarked cynically. "It's not a particularly good Rühmann film, but in wartime, it serves its purpose."

Rühmann himself never publicly commented on the implicit political messages of the films he made in the Third Reich. His rather tedious autobiography ignores the topic altogether, describing *Quax* as a "movie entirely in the spirit of my love of flying," Rühmann's hobby. On the other hand, it would be incorrect to say Rühmann was a die-hard Nazi. He didn't especially curry favor with the Nazi leadership, but neither did he try to distance himself from those in power. An Allied committee after the war concluded that he was a conformist who had let himself be blown along in the prevailing winds of the Nazi era—an accurate assessment of Rühmann's political passivity. That he continued to make films in Nazi Germany although his wife, Maria Bernheim, was Jewish and his friend Otto Wallburg was forced into exile and then murdered shows timidity, tunnel vision, and careerism, but not necessarily any sympathy with Nazi ideology.

Rühmann biographer Torsten Körner has pointed out that the actor did not owe his success to any one political system. His ability to embody the "little man on the street" had already made him a star in the Weimar Republic, and he retained his popularity after Hitler and Goebbels fell. His attitude toward the two Nazi leaders, who furthered his career, must have been ambivalent at best. Surely he would have been shocked when the propaganda minister called upon him to divorce his wife, and any sympathies he may have had for the Nazi Party could hardly have been increased when the SS organ *Das Schwarze Korps* pilloried him for being married to a "full-blown Jewess." Against this backdrop of threats, he compromised, never daring to break with the regime that tried to impinge to such an extent on his personal life.

Following Göring's advice, he divorced Bernheim and arranged a fake marriage for her with Swedish actor Rolf von Nauckhoff, to whom he gave a sports car as an expression of his gratitude. Bernheim was allowed to emigrate to Sweden, where she spent the war safe and sound. Since Rühmann's marriage had been on the rocks anyway, one can hardly accuse him of behaving improperly, especially as he paid her a generous monthly alimony. Later, when he got remarried, to the actress Hertha Feiler, he invited Maria to his wedding. The Nazi elite probably weren't all that thrilled that the new wife of Germany's beloved comedy star was a "quarter Jewess," but this time there were no consequences. The authorities gritted their teeth and remained silent.

Nonetheless, there was much that was contradictory in Rühmann's personal and career choices. On the one hand, he once tried—in vain—to intervene to prevent the execution of an acquaintance. On the other, he lent his talents to more than one morally dubious film, including *The Gas Man*, a 1939 movie in which he played a low-level civil servant who gets caught up in the machinery of Nazi legal system. The real message of the film, which purported to be a light comedy, was that those who didn't play ball with the system would get punished. In the first act of the film, a stranger gives Rühmann's character some money. Rühmann is suspicious and tries to report the incident but ends up being sent to answer for himself at the office for Aryan identification. Having tried to do the right thing, he then decides to spend the money, but his new life of luxury attracts suspicion, and he is called in for Gestapo interrogation. In the end, a court discovers that the whole affair is a harmless prank, and Rühmann is acquitted instead of being sentenced to death for betraying his responsibility to the state.

This "light entertainment" makes for fairly creepy, not to say uncanny, viewing today. The party elite didn't like it—they disapproved of the inclusion of so many everyday details about the Nazi state, and *The Gas Man* was rarely screened. The state film studio UFA even had to cut a scene, at the insistence of deputy head of the Nazi party Rudolf Hess, in which Rühmann performed an unacceptably sloppy Hitler salute. Rühmann himself clearly did not enjoy participating in overly propagandistic films and tried to avoid being conscripted into battle on the entertainment front. Whenever he was called upon to propagate Nazi ideology, he tried to keep his appearance brief. But despite his efforts not to be co-opted into the regime, he maintained a close friendship with Ernst Udet, a Nazi Luftwaffe commander, who shared his passion for flying. In the middle of wartime, Rühmann was allowed to continue flying as a hobby pilot—a rare privilege. The relationship between Germany's most famous comedian and the Nazi leadership remained enigmatic. Certainly, he had no one but himself to blame for the post-war accusations he faced that he had actively supported the Third Reich.

BUT THE NAZI entertainment industry produced films that were far less appetizing than even *The Gas Man*—or than the Wehrmacht comedy *Concert by Request*, in which Rühmann made a fleeting appearance. The absolute nadir was Hans H. Zerlett's anti-Semitic musical *Robert and Bertram*. Based on a Gustav Raeder farce that had not been anti-Jewish, the story revolved around the adventures of a pair of vagabonds, played by the comedians Rudi Godden and Kurt Seifert. They meet a German girl named Lenchen whose father wants to marry her against her will to one of his creditors. Lenchen is in love with a handsome fellow named Michel, and in order to save her, the two vagabonds sneak into a costume party held by Commercial Councilor Ipelmeyer, a Jew, and steal the family jewelry. Since Ipelmeyer's gains are ill-gotten, this is not viewed as a crime. Lenchen's father is able to pay off his debts, and the overjoyed girl gets to marry her beloved Michel.

The film's slender plot was merely a pretense to run the gamut of anti-Semitic clichés. Ipelmeyer, who with his crooked nose looks like a *Stürmer* caricature, constantly lusts after the ballet dancers at his costume party and makes a series of sordid advances. His servant, played by Robert Dorsay, accompanies the proceedings with a stream of idiotic commentary in pseudo-Yiddish. Ipelmeyer's obese wife waddles through the tasteless luxury of their mansion, and the banker's various friends are equally repulsive figures. Zerlett, the director, boasted in an interview about the film's "strong anti-Semitic tendency," adding, "Of course, the six featured Jewish roles had to be played by non-Jews, but the makeup is so lifelike that no one will doubt that my Semites are genuine."

Zerlett's remarks were published in the magazine *Film-Kurier* on January 17, 1939, roughly two months after the Kristallnacht pogrom. Film historian Klaus Kreimeier has rightly called *Robert and Bertram* an "advertisement for death," and it's hard to interpret Zerlett's sorry excuse for a movie as anything else. It was made around the same time as the notoriously anti-Semitic historical drama *Jud Süss*, a huge popular hit, and it wasn't long before cattle cars full of deported Jews began rolling eastward. The Final Solution had begun, and the connection between the flood of anti-Semitic films and genocide can hardly be denied. Kreimeier writes:

> The fact that by 1942 this genre had run its course can be attributed to the fact that the killing machinery was running at full speed. Propaganda had done its job. The Nazi leadership had to have assumed that the mass deportations would not go unnoticed by the general populace, and the mass exterminations were probably a public secret. But thanks to factors that included a series of several very successful films, the German people had been psychologically prepared. That, in any case, was how the

political leadership and their minions in the film industry saw the situation.

The distorted image of Jewishness at the center of *Robert and
Bertram*'s comic plot was not just a reflection of crude beer-tent
anti-Semitism. It was part of a coolly planned, larger strategy. A
seemingly harmless comedy was a far more effective means of
infusing poisonous propaganda than the weekly newsreels. Audiences laughed and did not expect any political message. But the
humor in question made them receptive to the campaigns that
led to the persecution, ostracism, and extermination of Jews.

V. HUMOR AND WAR

AFTER A FEW YEARS of deceptive calm, during which the German leadership continued to assure the world of its peaceful intentions, developments came fast and furious. In the initial phase of German expansion, Hitler achieved bloodless victories that bolstered his fantasies of omnipotence. He annexed Austria and met no resistance. Girls holding flowers and other newly-found citizens of the Third Reich greeted German troops with cheers; the people who received German citizenship on Vienna's Heldenplatz were eager to take part in what looked to be a great National Socialist adventure. But soon the arrogance with which faraway Berlin ruled over their country reawakened old feelings of inferiority toward their much bigger neighbor. The Nazis installed Josef Bürkel as their district leader in Vienna— an alcoholic party hack from the Rhine who neither understood nor wanted to understand Austrians. The Viennese soon dubbed Bürkel the "beer director," and amongst themselves began to speak insultingly of all Germans. Still, despite such frictions, the Nazis achieved 99 percent of the Austrian vote in a referendum on the annexation.

Franz Dannimann's compilation of wartime jokes includes a piece of graffiti that appeared on the sides of buildings in the Austrian capital: "Only the dumbest calves elect their own slaughterers." But the vast majority of Austrians had willingly sacrificed their homeland—as far as they did view the Austrian state, created in 1918, as a homeland—on the altar of Greater German nationalism. They only recovered from their intoxication with the onset of World War II and the prospect of their own demise.

Nonetheless, some jokes that survive provide evidence of wounded national pride—the predominant theme in Austrian political humor under Hitler:

> *After the annexation, a Nazi district leader visits a school in Linz, where the students have carefully rehearsed questions and answers. The district leader calls on little Seppl Ebeseder: "Who is your father?" "Adolf Hitler." "Who is your mother?" "Greater Germany." "Very good! And what do you want to be when you grow up?" "An orphan."*

What popular Austrian humor ignored, however, were the violent anti-Semitic pogroms that commenced immediately after the annexation. Jewish professors were forced to clean street gutters with toothbrushes, and while the cultured elements in the Austrian populace did not laugh at such instances of humiliation, many took part in cruelties meted out to Jews.

This terrible persecution was directed precisely at those Jewish citizens who had done the most to enrich Austrian society. Among the victims of the public harassment and waves of arrests were the cream of Austrian cabaret. On the day before German troops marched in, Fritz Grünbaum had mounted the stage of the Simpl Theater, where a short circuit had knocked out the lights, with the words: "I see nothing, absolutely nothing. I must have stumbled into Nazi cultural policies." Twenty-four hours later, the comedian was running for his life. But his plan to seek refuge in Czechoslovakia was thwarted when the border was closed. His former stage partner, Karl Farkas, tried to persuade him to make a second attempt, but Grünbaum refused. Farkas escaped alone.

And on May 7, 1938, the flagship Nazi newspaper *Der Volkische Beobachter* reported, "We've got Grünbaum." The cabaret comic, the paper went on, would now have an opportunity to "revisit all the jokes he made." They meant in Dachau.

While the noose was gradually tightening around Jews' necks in Austria, Nazi officials in Berlin were feverishly preparing new acts of infamy elsewhere. So far, German expansion had been bloodless, but now the German economy was being prepared for a second phase: bloody wars of conquest. The Nazis raised the funds needed for armaments by collecting taxes and through its Winter Relief Fund (Winterhilfswerk), which was supposed to go for economic stimulus and social programs. Germans may have believed they were saving up to buy one of the newly introduced Volkswagens, but Hitler was also using their savings to build tanks. Göring was charged with drawing up an economic Four-Year Plan, but instead of bolstering the civilian sector, he spent the money at his disposal on 3,300 warplanes.

The populace was not compensated for the financial sacrifices they made with any visible social benefits, and eventually it became clear that there was something fishy going on, as the following quip illustrates:

What should the German people use to keep warm, if the Four-Year Plan stipulates that wood is needed for more important tasks? The answer is simple. We'll clothe ourselves in a cozy new textile made from the cobwebs in Hitler's brain, the webs of lies told by Goebbels, and the delicate thread of the German people's patience.

That patience was constantly being tried by Nazi appeals for voluntary donations. But the money collected door to door by so-called charities like the Winter Relief Fund mysteriously disappeared. Some people scoffed that Catholicism and National Socialism had finally discovered something in common:

The Catholics say: pray every morning, pray every noon, pray every evening. The National Socialist says: Pay every morning, pay every noon, pay every evening.

Others joked that Volkswagens' indicator lights should be made out of Winter Relief Fund donation cans—people were always quick to get out of the way of those.

Yet despite Hitler's rearmament programs and his unscrupulous, vampire-like sucking at the people's pockets, the Führer led Germany into war only half prepared, and even a half-committed response from the West might well have spelled the end of the Nazi empire before it began. The strength Hitler liked to project abroad grotesquely belied the actual power structure in Europe in 1939. Hitler's power was simply the power of suggestion, but it had the desired effect. None of the political principals at the time realized that when he flexed his muscles he was bluffing.

The only sign of the enormous pressure the Führer had put himself under and his fear that he might have overplayed his hand was a new exaggerated animosity toward critics and pessimists. Hitler's sudden sensitivity, itself an indication of his frayed nerves, had dire consequences for those who laughed at his expense. "The making of political jokes is a useless remnant of liberalism," Goebbels wrote in the *Völkischer Beobachter*. Ever the attentive servant of his master, the propaganda minister had noticed how thin-skinned the Führer had become.

Those cabaret artists who had remained in the Third Reich had no idea a clampdown was coming. Having been miraculously released from a concentration camp, Werner Finck was performing at Berlin's Cabaret of Comedians, which was under the direction of Willy Schaeffers, who was known for toeing the party line. Schaeffers had hired Finck on condition that he refrain from political references in his act. Finck had sworn he would do exactly that, but began referring to his performance on stage as "half throttle"—a suggestion that his humor was being self-censored and that audiences should read between the lines.

In one sketch, for instance, a woman asked Finck for the time, to which he responded: "I'm not allowed to talk about that." That drew a grin form the audience, who knew the comedian had been muzzled. Finck also made sly references to the general dangers of speaking one's mind under a repressive regime with party spies potentially lurking everywhere. One of his favorite jokes was:

> *A guy goes to the dentist, who says, "Open your mouth, please." The guy answers, "No way. I don't even know you."*

Nazi apparatchiks soon got wind of the fact that Finck was implicitly criticizing the government gag he had supposedly accepted. In January 1939, "cultural inspectors" who served as spies for the Propaganda Ministry reported that the state and the party were being openly mocked at the Cabaret of Comedians. Finck did not suspect the trouble he was in. Despite having received a few warnings, he was later to write, all seemed quiet on the "Goebbels front."

That quiet was deceptive: Goebbels, determined not to be flouted again by his rival Göring, was preparing a renewed attack on Finck within the General Staff. "Political jokes will be eradicated, ripped out by the very roots," Goebbels noted in his diary. The opening salvo of his campaign against humor was to strip

Finck and three colleagues of membership in the Imperial Cultural Chamber and forbid them to ever work again. The reason given in the official justification was that they "lacked any positive attitude toward National Socialism." The severity of this blow completely surprised Finck, who now also worried, not without justification, that he would be sent back to a concentration camp.

As 1939 wore on, he learned from confidential sources inside the Propaganda Ministry that old scores were about to be settled and he was to be removed from society altogether. He knew he had to act quickly and decisively. With a new world war already in full swing, going into exile was no longer an option. How could the comedian escape the bloodhounds of the powerful Goebbels, whom he had so terribly angered? Finck decided that the best defense was a good offense and volunteered for the military.

This clever maneuver put him beyond the reach of the Propaganda Ministry, but not other perils. Not only could Finck have been killed by the enemy, he also had to watch his tongue among his fellow troops, given the rules, instituted in 1938, concerning "defeatism" among the ranks. This legislation, which bore the bureaucratic title "Wartime Special Punishment Ordinance," was the brainchild of Field Marshal Wilhelm Keitel, a sycophantic devotee of Hitler. It essentially gave the Nazis *carte blanche* to murder anyone they defined as "opposition." According to paragraph 5, the punishment for "undermining the armed forces" was death—that is, those who questioned the war or made defeatist or critical statements could be put before a firing squad. (Women offenders were to be guillotined—ostensibly at the express request of the Führer.) The criterion for determining who was undermining or acting to the detriment of the war effort was "healthy popular sense." The authorities took the measure of that, so they could be completely arbitrary. The ordinance was another means of tightening the screws and keeping people in fear of the totalitarian state.

THE THIN SKINS of the Nazi leadership and their harsh laws against criticism and defeatism reflected the fact that they had a hard time getting Germans enthused about the war. The veterans of World War I knew only too well the horrors of a two-front conflict. Most Germans felt uneasy about Hitler's plans for the invasion of Poland, an act that would lead to a military confrontation with England and France. Morale was poor, despite the constant barrage of propaganda. Heinz Rühmann had landed a hit with the upbeat ditty "Nothing Scares a Seaman," which people sang and whistled on every street corner. But whether that song really kept Germans holding on throughout World War II, as it was later credited with doing, is an open question. In any case, the Nazis could not force the people to break out in wild hurrays over going to war. The fearful memories of Verdun lay too deep for that.

So the leadership decided instead to pull in the reins and silence critical voices, if necessary, by legally sanctioned murder. But the people, shocked by so many ominous developments, one following on the heels of another, could not completely hold their tongues. Hitler's mad foreign policy maneuvers and the popular suspicion that war was becoming inevitable caused a surprising number of Germans to shake their heads and even to quit the Nazi Party.

For years, the Nazi leadership had tried to curry favor with England to clear the way for an unopposed conquest of territory in Eastern Europe, but Hitler's overtures had yielded nothing but a minor naval treaty. Furious at being rebuffed by these stubborn English, and driven by mistaken tactical considerations, the

Führer decided instead to treaty with his ideological archenemy, the Soviet Union. For decades, he had ranted and raved about the Bolshevik threat. But in 1939 he threw his principles out the window for the sole purpose of avoiding a two-front war while he overran Poland. The Soviet Non-Aggression Pact—which Hitler would scrap two years later—actually encouraged the Western European powers to resolve on a full-force strike at the next act of war perpetrated by Germany. In the short term, Hitler's pact with Stalin temporarily staved off the need to fight on two fronts, but in the long term, it would lead to military catastrophe.

Military consequences notwithstanding, this rapprochement with an enemy made it difficult for Hitler to explain his actions to his own people, and a number of popular jokes went the rounds questioning the Führer's credibility:

Hitler's gift to [Soviet Foreign Minister] Molotov at the signing of the Non-Aggression Pact was an autographed edition of Mein Kampf *with editorial changes made by the Führer himself. He crossed out all the anti-Russian bits.*

A similar joke played on the meaning of the words *mein Kampf*—"my battle": Stalin was planning to write an autobiography, *Your Battle, My Victory.* The joke called to mind the fact that under the Non-Aggression Pact, the Soviet Union would get the eastern half of Poland.

The official state propaganda machine paid such sarcastic jokes little regard and continued to praise the unholy alliance with Stalin as an act of strategic genius. The pact essentially divided up the spoils before the victory. It was clear that real deeds would have to follow Hitler's diplomatic somersaults. Events had developed a fatal dynamic of their own. A joke that made the round before the start of World War II accurately anticipated what was to follow:

It's July 1939, and three Swiss are talking about where they want to go on vacation. They agree that it's time to see Germany. One says he wants to go to Munich, and the second says he'd like to visit Berlin. The third pipes up: "I'm going to Warsaw. "But Warsaw isn't part of Germany," the other two object. The third says: "My vacation's in October."

The man who recorded this joke, Ralph Wiener, correctly notes that it contains an element of Nazi wish fulfillment. And it's likely that its author was convinced of the propriety of a German attack on Poland. In any case, the joke is evidence of German megalomania, an attitude that had begun to take root in the new fascist popular community. The earlier uneasy reaction to Hitler's bellicose posturing had not been based on moral objections but on fears that the trauma of 1918 would be repeated. That concern was finally wiped away by Nazi Germany's successful campaign against France in 1940. The vast majority of Germans basked in that bloody triumph. But their glee at the success of Germany's blitzkrieg was short-lived. The attack on Poland had isolated Germany from the community of nations. Germany fought largely alone in its war against the rest of the world. Its biggest ally was Italy, hardly a military powerhouse.

In fact, the Nazis had trouble cementing their partnership with Europe's other main fascist dictatorship. Initially, Mussolini was extremely skeptical about Hitler's ambitions, in particular the Führer's plan to form Germans into a "racially pure herd." The event that forged the alliance was the second Italo-Abyssinian war, a brutal and hopelessly anachronistic colonial endeavor for which Hitler provided raw materials. The German populace did not fail to note the attempts of the two regimes to come together. In one popular joke, Göring is sent to Abyssinia and telegraphs back to Berlin: "Emperor has fled—stop—his uniform fits me—stop—Hermann."

Mussolini repaid Hitler for his support by accepting Germany's annexation of Austria without protest, and by 1939, shortly before the start of World War II, the relationship between the two states had flourished to the point where Italy agreed to a "pact of steel" that bound it militarily to Germany without restriction. Foolishly, Mussolini promised to join his larger ally in the event of any kind of warfare, offensive as well as defensive. With a single stroke of the pen, he sealed his own fate, although afterward he seems to have realized how carelessly he had thrown in his lot with the warmongering Führer. In any case, despite the pact, signed at the time with martial decisiveness, Italy did not take part in Germany's campaign against Poland, and Mussolini only participated in hostilities against France once it became clear that Hitler would emerge victorious. Mussolini sent the first troops to France one week before the *grande nation* capitulated, and while German tank divisions were rolling toward Paris, Italian soldiers were straggling in the suburbs of Menton, on the French-Italian border.

Mussolini, who had hoped to receive a part of France as a reward for this timely assistance, was promptly nicknamed "the imperial harvest helper." In the eyes of many Germans, Italy was a completely unreliable and opportunistic ally. Wisecrackers sneered that Mussolini had declared of Gaul: "I came when I saw that he had conquered." But Italy stood by Germany throughout the rest of the war, plunging with its ally into the abyss. To make up for his past failings, Mussolini supported every one of Hitler's subsequent murderous ventures, although he was motivated less by bad conscience or concern about his reputation than by his own fantastical dreams and boundless greed. He believed that all of Europe would become fascist, and he wanted a big piece of the pie.

In 1940, Italian troops invaded Greece, but soon ran into difficulties and had to be rescued from defeat by hastily deployed German units. That only confirmed German prejudices about the weakness of the Southern European mentality and provided fodder for a further series of jokes, like this one:

> When the Wehrmacht High Command received word that Italy had joined the war, one general opined, "That will cost us an extra ten divisions." When informed that Italy was fighting on Germany's side, he sighed, "Ouch, make that twenty."

There was good reason to regard Italy as a military featherweight, although it had nothing to do with Southern European mentality. The modest might of the Italian army aside, Germany's ally only went to war begrudgingly. Except for Mussolini, no one in the Italian ruling class was very enthusiastic—neither the king nor the military nor the industrial leadership supported Il Duce's military adventure. One untranslatably obscene joke in Germany had Mussolini ordering the removal of toilets from Italian rail cars because "the Italians don't give a shit about the Axis." That punch line was an accurate assessment of the morale among Italian troops.

Most German jokes against their ally, however, revolved around the idea that the only thing Italy's military did well was retreat. One joke, common among German soldiers, played upon the Italian tendency to call in help when things went wrong:

> *In Italy there's a new dance craze. It's called the Retreat and*
> *it goes like this: You take one step forward, then two steps*
> *back, spin around your axis, and hide behind your partner.*

But after their own initial series of triumphs, German troops didn't have much luck themselves, and there was little reason to point fingers at their weaker ally.

The German campaign against England, in particular, failed to yield any notable success. The air battles, which Germany hoped would establish its superiority in the skies, ended in a fiasco. The strategy developed by Göring, who was in charge of the Luftwaffe, simply didn't work, and bombarding civilian targets in English cities only strengthened English resolve. This was all the more true in 1940 when Winston Churchill replaced the indecisive Neville Chamberlain. Churchill's "Blood, sweat and tears" speech lent European opposition to Hitler a powerful voice and bolstered the morale of Britons, who set about turning their nation into a fortress. Hitler was repeatedly forced to postpone Operation Sea Lion, the planned German invasion of the British Isles.

Jokers among the German populace quickly noticed that, in the case of England, Hitler could not follow up his bellicose posturing with action:

> *After defeating France, Hitler stands by the English Chan-*
> *nel, gazing over at the enemy and wondering why an inva-*
> *sion is proving so difficult. Suddenly, Moses appears next*
> *to him and says: "If you hadn't persecuted my people, I*
> *would have showed you the trick I used to part the Red*
> *Sea." Hitler's bodyguards arrest him and torture him until*

he confesses, "I only need to hold the staff God gave me over the water, and the waves will recede." "So where is this staff," *Hitler screams. "Give it to me!" Moses shrugs and says: "It's in the British Museum."*

In Churchill, Hitler had found an adversary as determined as he was. Nonetheless, most Germans weren't worried about their military prospects during the first half of World War II. On the contrary, the speed with which the Nazi Empire was growing infused even hardcore skeptics with enthusiasm for the conflict. Only a very few were worried that German strength was being dispersed in a variety of offensive wars or felt concern that German death squads pursued their malevolent work in the countries that had capitulated.

One of these few was the first person to try to assassinate Hitler. The Munich-born clockmaker Georg Elser was a pacifist with unusual prescience who saw where Hitler's megalomania would lead and tried to kill the Führer with a bomb made from stolen dynamite. Acting alone, Elser detonated the device on November 8, 1939, at a large Nazi Party event in Munich's Bürgerbräukeller, where Hitler was the main speaker. The attempt failed because Hitler had shortened his speech in order to catch a train to Berlin and had already left the building.

Ironically, many Germans believed the bombing was another stunt staged by the Nazis themselves. Kurt Sellin, who published the first postwar collection of wartime German jokes, recorded the following quip:

The attempted assassination of Hitler in the Bürgerbräukeller left 10 people dead, 50 injured, and 60 million fooled.

It seems strange that Germans would interpret a bombing in which several high-ranking Nazis were killed as an attempt by the party to put one over on the populace. On the other hand, there was little Germans thought Hitler incapable of, including killing his own comrades, so perhaps their suspicions were sincere. Many people regarded the Night of the Long Knives and even the Reichstag fire as Nazi propaganda spectacles. In this case, however, they were mistaken. The assassination attempt had been genuine, the work of a single man of conscience. Elser was quickly arrested and sent to Dachau, where he was murdered in 1944, when his contemporaries had finally begun to see clearly, as he had long before, the infernal path that Hitler had chosen to go down. But in 1940 the vast majority of Germans were intoxicated by Hitler's early military success, and Elser's would long remain the only attempt to assassinate the Führer.

When Hitler attacked the Soviet Union in 1941, more people began to see dark clouds on the horizon. Even Rudolf Hess, Hitler's deputy, felt that extreme steps were now necessary to avoid a two-front war. Shortly after the launch of Hitler's suicidal Operation Barbarossa in Eastern Europe, Hess, on his own initiative, decided to negotiate a peace deal with England. On May 10, 1941, he commandeered a plane and flew to Scotland, where he was immediately arrested. It was a crazy thing to do, the act of an unstable man who had lost all sense of reality, and Hess's precise motivation remains unclear to this day. When Hitler learned of what his deputy had done, he declared Hess mentally ill and issued an order that he be shot—should he ever return to Germany.

The German people had their own, comic take on Hess's exploit. One joke has Churchill greeting Hess, "So you're the madman," to which Hess responds, "No, I'm just his deputy." (In reality, Hess never got to talk to the prime minister.) Other jokes played on the suspicion that Hess's real mission had been to flee Nazi Germany. A parody of a child's bedtime prayer ran: "Dear God, please make me crazy so I, too, can fly to Scotland." And wise-crackers alluding to the failure of Germany's strenuous efforts to conquer the British sneered that Hess was the only German who'd ever succeeded in invading England.

There was no end to the variety of jokes involving Hess as a lunatic in an age of collective lunacy, or as a madman who was the only German with a clear head. Previously, Hitler's unassuming deputy had attracted little attention; now, he was center stage, in the spotlight. Instead of delivering a peace deal, he had provided priceless fodder for wartime humor. This example is particularly macabre:

> Two old acquaintances run into one another in a concen-
> tration camp. "Why are you in here?" asks one. "On May
> 10, I said Rudolf Hess was crazy," the other answers, "and
> yourself?" "On May 15, I said Hess wasn't crazy."

This joke shows how aware Germans were in 1941 of the terrible power exercised by the Nazi state. But few rebelled against Nazi excesses, because of fear, indifference, or basic National Socialist convictions.

The signs were clear, however, that Nazi Germany had passed its zenith. In attacking its archenemy-turned–temporary ally to the east, Germany had overreached itself. The Soviet Union, with its vast territory and immense military resources, was a wall against which Hitler would bang his head for the next four years. Once again, Germany began by conquering territory, but within in a few months, its advances slowed and then stopped altogether. What followed was the darkest period of the Third Reich, and in that period an empire was radicalized, internally and externally, to an extent previously unknown in history.

LONG BEFORE Hitler proceeded to his Final Solution, people abroad knew that Jews were being cruelly discriminated against and persecuted in Germany. But it was not a topic much canvassed in the general culture of the world outside; for example, films of the prewar years made little mention of these injustices. In the age of appeasement, the political situation was too precarious for such accusations, and in the 1930s the only moviemaking nation to be truly active on the propaganda front was Germany itself. The most powerful world influence on public opinion, Hollywood, had little interest in producing films that were harshly critical of the Nazis, though the studios' reasons had less to do with political sympathies than with practical, economic considerations. Although few people wanted to admit it, the American film industry depended on the European market, and in a time haunted by fascist terrorism and fears of a new war, no one in Europe wanted to see "problem films." Audiences craved diversion, and Hollywood provided them with tailor-made escapist fantasies, light entertainment in every conceivable form.

The American people themselves maintained an embarrassed distance from the unruly, self-destructive nations of "Old Europe," and the problems of the European continent seemed especially far away to those basking in the southern California sun. In 1936, only five percent of Americans overall could conceive of their country going to war against Germany. And instead of telling the truth about Germany's rearmament and racist insanity, Hollywood had its stars doing dance steps. Only with the onset of World War II did the big studios begin to mobilize audiences.

Here, too, economic considerations played a major role. After the German invasion of Poland, the European market had drastically shrunk. Many films could not even be distributed within wartime Europe. Meanwhile the mood in America had turned patriotic, and even the calculating studio bosses began to realize that the United States might not be able to avoid entering World War II.

ONE STAR of the American film industry had recognized, much more quickly than his colleagues, just how dangerous the German threat was. Charlie Chaplin had been involved in World War I, too: with his film *Shoulder Arms*, the world's most famous comedian had marched to the front against the Kaiser's Imperial Germany. No one knew how to use humor as a weapon more perfectly than Chaplin, and he was born to create a cinematic parody of—and warning against—the absurdly inflated imagery of the Nazis.

A number of strange coincidences connected Chaplin with Hitler. Not only did they wear the same mustache, but also they were born only four days apart. Surprisingly, Chaplin did not come up with the idea of playing the role of the psychopathic dictator on his own; it was suggested to him by his fellow director and producer Alexander Korda. In his memoir, Chaplin described his reaction to Korda's suggestion :

And now another war was brewing and I was trying to write a story for Paulette [Goddard]; but I could make no progress. How could I throw myself into feminine whimsy or think of romance or the problems of love when madness was being stirred up by a hideous grotesque—Adolf Hitler?

Alexander Korda in 1937 had suggested I should do a Hitler story based on mistaken identity, Hitler having the same mustache as the tramp: I could play both characters, he said. I did not think too much about the idea then, but now it was topical, and I was desperate to get working again. Then it suddenly struck me. Of course! As Hitler I could harangue the crowds in jargon and talk all I wanted to. And as the tramp I could remain more or less silent. A Hitler story was an opportunity for burlesque and pantomime. So with this enthusiasm I went hurrying back to Hollywood and set to work writing a script. The story took two years to develop.

Chaplin's ambitions were cemented by the fact that German journalists were constantly going after him in their propaganda organs, with Goebbels's press referring to him as "the little Jewish tumbling figure" or simply as "repulsive." Chaplin could hardly wait to pay the Nazis back for their insults.

The final script for *The Great Dictator* was completed the same day England declared war on Germany, and the project, in which Chaplin had already invested half a million dollars, went into production shortly thereafter. The story was simple but clever. Chaplin plays a Jewish barber who has lost his memory in World War I and is released from hospital after years of fruitless treatment, only to find Tomania (Germany) completely changed. The barber knows nothing about the political rise of the Nazis or their anti-Semitic pogroms, an ignorance that leads to a series of absurd situations. Chaplin also plays the megalomaniacal Tomanian dictator, Adenoid Hynkel, and the scene jumps back and forth between the ghetto and the autocrat's palace. Hynkel delivers a number of bizarre speeches to the masses in jumbled pseudo-German, bosses around his henchmen Herring (Göring) and Garbitsch (Goebbels), and engages in ridiculous competitions with his Italian ally and rival, Benzino Napaloni. Because the Jewish barber and the Tomanian dictator look exactly alike, the plot turns into a comedy of mistaken identities. The barber takes over Hynkel's office, sends the tyrant to a concentration camp, and makes a speech pleading for peace and lambasting the misanthropic, racist policies of his doppelganger. A scene from the first draft of the script that showed the dictator's Jewish wife undergoing cosmetic surgery in order to look like a stereotypical German Frau was left out because it was considered too drastic.

Chaplin immersed himself in his work on the set. He had viewed copious material from the weekly German newsreels and sucked up details like a sponge. In order to play both roles equally plausibly, he shot the Hynkel and barber scenes at separate times, first tackling the ghetto sequences before moving on to the ones in the dictator's palace, which he filmed in December 1939. By March 1940, he was able to inform his studio bosses that the movie was a wrap. There had been worrisome signals from the U.S. State Department while the film was being shot, and the appeasement-era British government, too, fretted that a film depicting Hitler as a buffoon might not be such a good idea and threatened to ban it from being shown in the U.K. Chaplin had legitimate reason to be concerned the film might never see the light of day.

But then events took a dramatic turn, as Chaplin later described in his autobiography:

Before I had finished *The Dictator* England declared war on the Nazis. I was in Catalina on my boat over the weekend and heard the depressing news over the radio. In the beginning there was inaction on all fronts. "The Germans will never break through the Maginot Line," we said. Then suddenly the holocaust began: the breakthrough in Belgium, the collapse of the Maginot Line, the stark and ghastly fact of Dunkirk—and France was occupied. The news was growing gloomier. England was fighting with her back to the wall. Now our New York office was wiring frantically, "Hurry up with your film, everyone is waiting for it."

The Nazi government launched a full-scale diplomatic campaign to stop Chaplin's project at the last minute. But although many Americans still sympathized with Germany, its efforts were in vain.

Chaplin's troubles, however, were far from over. Before the film's premiere, he received letters from people who threatened to throw stink bombs or even shoot bullets at the screen. He went ahead anyway, and the film was a huge popular hit, making more money than any of the comedian's other movies. The press was less enthusiastic; some critics accused Chaplin of throwing his lot in with the Communists. Many objected in particular to the sentimental speech by the Jewish barber at the end of the film, addressed directly to the audience. The naive pacifism it expressed was probably what led Chaplin to cautiously distance himself from *The Great Dictator* after World War II. He later said that if he had known then the extent of the Nazis' crimes, including Auschwitz, he would have never made the movie.

Ernst Lubitsch, the director of the other great anti-Nazi wartime comedy, would receive none of the laurels enjoyed by Chaplin. In fact, *To Be or Not to Be*, which is today rightly regarded as a classic, caused him substantial difficulties. Above all, it was bad timing that caused audiences to reject and critics to lambast the film. Chaplin's *Great Dictator* hit the cinemas in 1940, well before the United States entered the war. It was easy for people in the U.S. to laugh at the terrible events in Europe when the conflict still seemed so far away. But a year later, when Lubitsch began shooting his masterpiece, the situation had changed. The Stars and Stripes now flew over the battlefields of Europe and American blood was being shed to help free the world of the terror of Nazism, and that was no laughing matter. For many, it was a completely inappropriate time to release a comedy about the Third Reich.

But although critics and public resisted the idea behind it, *To Be or Not to Be* was a very funny film. The plot was a twisted work of genius. A young Polish fighter pilot, Stanislav Sobinski (Robert Stack), falls in love with the theater actress Maria Tura (Carole Lombard). Every time Tura's actor husband takes the stage and launches into the famous Hamlet soliloquy, Sobinski leaves the audience and has a backstage rendezvous with Tura. Just as their affair is discovered, World War II breaks out, and Sobinski leaves his lover to go fight. When it becomes clear that Poland is no match for the more powerful Germany, he travels on to London, where he and other exiles volunteer to fly dangerous missions for the Royal Air Force. But a Gestapo spy called Professor Siletzsky has insinuated his way into the ranks of the Poles fighting in exile, and by a simple ruse, he gets his hands on a complete list of individuals active in the Polish resistance. On that list is Maria Tura, and when the unsuspecting Sobinski asks Siletzsky to pass on the words "To be or not to be" to her, the fake professor misinterprets this as code. The pilot discovers Siletzsky's true identity, but not before the latter has made his way to Poland to hand over the list to an SS officer named Ehrhardt. Sobinski sets off to avert the catastrophe and parachutes into occupied Warsaw.

There he contacts Maria. Her troupe is distressed by the bad news but has no idea how they can prevent Siletzsky from passing the list with Maria's name to the Nazis. Sobinski and she then come up with a daring plan. They convert their theater into a fake Nazi headquarters and set a trap for Siletzsky. The actors dress up as Nazis, and Maria's husband Joseph takes the role of Gruppenführer Ehrhardt. The deception works, but during a conversion between the supposed Ehrhardt and Siletzsky it emerges that the spy has made a copy of the list, which he has left in his hotel room. So Joseph assumes a new role: the Gestapo spy Siletzsky. As the situation in Warsaw begins to heat up, the Turas dress up another actor as Hitler and flee with the entire troupe in the Führer's private plane.

Lubitsch approached the material with light hand and effortlessly mastered all the somersaults of the plot. The cast—especially Jack Benny, who plays the pompous thespian Joseph Tura—obviously had fun with the script. But the first screenings in early 1942 made it abundantly clear that the movie was going to flop. The specially invited audience greeted the clever punch lines with steely silence. In particular, many viewers were enraged a scene in which the real Ehrhardt says, "What [Tura] did to Shakespeare, we are now doing to Poland." Reviews were constantly citing this line as proof of how tasteless the film was, and whole rows of viewers left movie theaters when it was uttered. A wave of outrage was aimed at Lubitsch, who was accused of laughing at Polish suffering.

The following review illustrates the critics' incomprehension and knee-jerk rejection of the film:

Frankly, this corner is unable even remotely to comprehend the humor—or possibly the satire—in such a juxtaposition of fancy and fact. Where is the point of contact between an utterly artificial plot and the anguish of a nation which is one of the greatest tragedies of our time? What is the element of mirth in the remark which a German colonel makes regarding Mr. Benny's acting: "What he did to Shakespeare, we are doing now to Poland?" Even if one were able to forget the present horror which this implies, the butchery of a people would hardly be a matter for jest. Yet all the way through this picture runs a strange imperception of feeling. You might almost think Mr. Lubitsch had the attitude of "Anything for a laugh."

And this brings us back to the question: what is the conception behind a film that trades so distastefully upon the grim human tragedy now in effect? Why should a Hollywood producer endeavor to give significance to a fanciful tale by pretending that it is connected to the real events of today? Why, if he wants to make a picture with a story of such incredible proportions, should he not set it off in the realm of absolute make-believe?

Judging by what we have seen, the answer which stares us in the face is that some people in Hollywood still see the world through theatrical eyes. So deeply accustomed have they become to reflecting illusions and story patterns, not life, that the drama of current events becomes mere grist to their image-grinding mills. Poland, France, England and soon Wake Island are just locales for their same old story lines. Civilizations may crumble— but the hero and heroine come out all right in the end.

The *Philadelphia Inquirer* was even more drastic in its dispraise,

and, ironically, there was an anti-Semitic component to its negative review. Lubitsch, the critic wrote, was a jaded Jewish director.

To this day, *To Be or Not to Be* retains its stigma of tasteless-
ness in the American popular consciousness. Contemporary film
historians may be far milder in their judgments about Lubitsch's
work than the critics of his own day, but the moral objections to it
persist—with many viewers still finding some scenes inappropriate in light of the Nazi genocide in Eastern Europe.

Lubitsch himself was mortified by the harsh commentary of
his contemporaries, but he refused to cut the offending Shake-
speare-Poland joke. Instead, he mounted a vigorous defense of his
work in the American and British press. It took him two years to
react to the particular hostility directed at him by the *Inquirer*, but
when the same reviewer panned his next movie, Lubitsch submitted a long, well-argued open letter:

> I am not writing this letter with the intention to make
> you reconsider your criticism—nothing is farther from
> my mind. I am merely writing this letter to point out to
> you that several times in your criticism you resort to what
> one calls in sports circles a "foul."
>
> The purpose becomes very clear when in the next
> sentence in regard to *To Be or Not to Be* you call attention
> to my "callous, tasteless effort to find fun in the bombing
> of Warsaw."
>
> Being an experienced newspaper woman you are
> surely aware of the effect such an allegation must have on
> the reading public, particularly at a time like this. Such
> propaganda is not very gracious, but when it is based on
> false facts it becomes outrageous.
>
> Naturally, your statement that I "find fun in the

bombing of Warsaw" is completely untrue. When in *To Be or Not to Be* I have referred to the destruction of Warsaw I have shown it in all seriousness; the commentary under the shots of the devastated Warsaw speaks for itself and cannot leave any doubt in the spectator's mind what is my point of view and attitude towards those acts of horror. What I have satirized in this picture are the Nazis and their ridiculous ideology. I have also satirized the attitude of actors who always remain actors regardless of how dangerous the situation might be, which I believe is a true observation.

Never have I said in a picture anything derogative about Poland or the Poles. On the contrary I have portrayed them as a gallant people who do not cry on other people's shoulders in their misery but even in the darkest day never lost courage and ingenuity or their sense of humor.

It can be argued if the tragedy of Poland realistically portrayed as in *To Be or Not to Be* can be merged with satire. I believe it can be, and so did the audience which I observed during a screening of *To Be or Not to Be*; but this is a matter of debate and everyone is entitled to his point of view, but it is certainly a far cry from "the Berlin born director who finds fun in the bombing of Warsaw."

It is doubtful how effective Lubitsch's missive was, given the emotionally charged atmosphere of wartime America. It wasn't until after his death that *To Be or Not To Be* achieved the status of a classic.

Contemporary critics were unable to see beyond their own immediate horizons, which was why *The Great Dictator* and *To Be or Not To Be* were measured with different yardsticks. Nazis were supposed to be portrayed as teeth-baring monsters, and Poles as helpless victims—no other depictions were permissible. Lubitsch ignored such clichés. His Nazis were grotesque petty bureaucrats, and his Poles were clever Davids who put one over on the Goliath Hitler with their inventive tricks. Although the plot of *To Be or Not to Be* featured stock comic routines, the depiction of the Nazis as philistine lunkheads contained a truth that exceeded what was usually found in cinematic comedies. Lubitsch's biographer Herbert Spaich was right when he said that the director understood, much earlier than most of his contemporaries, the "banality of evil." Most of Hitler's henchmen were not demons. They were overly obedient petty bourgeois who had mutated into murderers. Their testimony about the Holocaust during the postwar trials showed that this view of the Nazis was largely correct. But America in 1942 was not ready for it.

RADIO PROGRAMS produced by the Allies had few qualms about making the Nazis look ridiculous. The BBC began German-language broadcasts in 1938, and the content was generated almost exclusively by German and Austrian émigrés. Estimates late in the war put the number of Germans who tuned in between 10 and 14 million. Listening to foreign radio was of course illegal, but the threat of punishment doesn't seem to have deterred many people.

It was a bold idea to combine news bulletins and swing music—which was very popular in Germany but had been banned by the Nazis—with satire. But the head of the BBC's German service, Robert Lukas, an Austrian Jew (born Robert Ehrenzweig, he had had emigrated in 1934), convinced his colleagues to give it a try.

They had no ethical qualms about poking fun at the Nazis or fears of being too inventive in doing it, and their first comedy show went over the airwaves in December 1940. The main character in the BBC's anti-Nazi satire was a private named Adolf Hirnschal, who reported back the news from the front to his "beloved wife." At times, Hirnschal's unit was surrounded, and at other times they were advancing against the Russians, and he refracted all the insanity of the war and of National Socialist ideology from his on-the-ground perspective. For every sacrifice he was called upon to make for the fatherland, he had a telling commentary.

Critically minded Germans who defied the law and tuned in to the BBC were delighted by these missives from England. The series featuring the fictional private who always said the first thing that popped into his head became a huge hit. The babbling, wisecracking Hirnschal would make his way through the remains of Europe right up until the end of the war, and the creative minds at the BBC used daily events as sources of inspiration.

For instance, the day after a failed attempt to assassinate Hitler at his Wolf's Lair retreat, Hirnschal sent an especially nonchalant letter home:

July 21, 1944

Dear Amalia, my beloved wife,
    You can't imagine the commotion among our ranks on account of the attack against our beloved Führer. Hans-Joachim Blitz said you can't believe how suddenly a twist of fate can happen. If the assassin had put his briefcase a foot-step to the right or the left, we'd perhaps be enjoying peace right now. But thankfully Divine Providence intervened. And as Blitz was saying this, First Lieutenant Hanke came

up and made a short speech, in which he explained that there had been a major miracle, and that it was proof that fate was on our side, and that the entire German people stood as one behind our beloved Führer, and that we would achieve victory with the help of the Führer and fate and our new V-rockets... Then there was an air-raid alarm, and immediately the bombs starting falling. One was a direct hit, and when we starting looking for the dead and wounded, we saw that poor Hans-Joachim Blitz's time was up. Jaschke and I stood in front of the body, and I said, "He may have walked with a limp, but he was a stand-up-straight guy." I had never seen anything like the expression of Jaschke's face before, as he said in a raspy voice, "Yep, that's the way it is. Today it's him. Tomorrow it may be me, and the day after that it could be you, Hirnschal." And I said: "Yep, Emil, that's the way it is. Tens of thousands who are alive today will die pitiful deaths. And many cities that today stand tall and lovely will be reduced to ash and rubble. And lots of women and children will starve to death or succumb to disease. And that's all because a briefcase was placed a footstep too far to the right or the left. If that's the way fate wanted it..."

And in that spirit, my beloved wife, you have my hugs and kisses,

> *Love, Adolf*
> *Private on the Western Front*

The success of the Hirnschal program inspired the BBC to try other satiric shows. Author Bruno Adler decided to go Private Hirnschal one better and came up with "Mrs. Wernicke," a

sharp-tongued, never-say-die Berlin woman who offered com-
monsense mockery of the coercive fascist state. She also subtly
advertised the BBC's German-language news programs. We can
only guess today how many Germans tuned into the shows created by Robert Lucas and his comedic cohorts.

The zenith of the BBC's satiric efforts came in 1940 when Austrian exile Johann Müller, who went by the pseudonym Martin
Miller, began parodying Hitler's bizarre speeches. Müller's Hitler
imitation was so perfect that the CIA is said to have asked the
British intelligence service MI6 what they thought of the Führer's
new pronouncements—referring to a Miller broadcast. Moreover, after the war, it emerged that this fake Hitler had attracted
a considerable German audience. A contemporary from Berlin,
Manfred Ormanowski, told of how his father, a Social Democrat,
transcribed and secretly reproduced Müller's Hitler speeches, using a basement printing press. Ormanowski himself distributed
the satiric leaflets to German critics of Hitler. He kept them hidden in the fake bottom of a fish tank and would visit friends of his
father ostensibly to swap fish, but actually to hand out the witty
pamphlets.

Müller's performances hardly convinced hardcore Nazis that
their ideology was ridiculous. But the BBC program did boost
the spirits of Hitler's German critics. As Ormanowski described
it, they felt as though they were not alone in their views. Müller knew that the best way to amuse his audience was to go after
Hitler where he was most vulnerable. After Hitler promised "final
victory" in 1941, for instance, Müller had the fake Führer hold a
year-in-review speech:

*My message today coincides with the conclusion of a year
in which I guaranteed final victory. But the year has only*

concluded according to the calendar, the same Gregorian calendar that was forced upon the Germanic world by international Jewry and a Roman pope named Gregor who had been bribed by Freemasons. Do we National Socialists, who have given the world a new order, want to be told by shadowy foreign forces when a year begins and when it ends? No, my racial comrades, I alone am entitled to decide when a year commences and when it concludes.

For the Nazi party, the highlights of the BBC's anti-Nazi satire initiative were unheard-of provocations, but the fascists were unskilled in the use of real humor as a weapon and came up with little in the way of a comic counterattack.

Ironically, earlier on in the war, it had looked as though the Nazis had an advantage on the propaganda front, and for a short time the English-language service of the German public radio broadcasters had almost as many listeners in England as the BBC. The broadcasts always began with "Germany calling," although the nasal voice of the announcer William Joyce made the words sound like "Jermany calling" and promptly earned the moderator the nickname Lord Haw-Haw. Instead of satire, the Nazis' English-language programming offered listeners cynical tips on how to treat injuries suffered in bombings. Joyce read out such advice in perfect Oxford English, though he was not at all an aristocrat, but rather an untamed thug with a large scar in his face that he'd received in a street fight. After the war, he was captured in Hamburg, where, as a former British citizen, he was executed for high treason.

DESPITE THE INITIAL propaganda inroads the Nazis made,

the BBC maintained the upper hand in the "radio war" until the demise of the Third Reich. Goebbels and his henchmen may have meted out draconian punishments to those found listening to foreign broadcasts, but such shows of force were an expression of helplessness. Even the gravest sanctions failed to deter Germans from secretly tuning in to the BBC. In 1939, for instance, a law was enacted making it a capital crime to pass on news from foreign broadcasters. The text of that piece of legislation left no doubt how seriously the Nazis took propaganda:

In modern warfare, the adversary does not fight only with military weapons, but also with instruments intended to influence and exhaust the people psychologically. One of these instruments is radio. Every word the adversary broadcasts is of course a lie conceived so as to harm the German people. The Imperial government knows that the German people are aware of this danger and consequently expects that every German will see it as a matter of responsibility and decency to avoid listening to foreign broadcasters. For those racial comrades who lack this sense of responsibility, the Council of Ministers for the Defense of the Empire has issued the following decree. The Council of Ministers for the Defense of the Empire has decided it shall be law for the entire territory of the Greater German Empire:

§1 It is prohibited to listen intentionally to foreign broadcasters. Violations will be punished with re-educational imprisonment. In milder cases, this can be reduced to mere incarceration. The radio receivers used will be confiscated.

§2 Whoever intentionally disseminates news from foreign broadcasters of the sort that may endanger the German people's capacity for resistance will be subject to re-educational incarceration and, in extreme cases, death.

But despite the number of spies among the populace and the unsavory show trials in which people were sentenced to death for violating this law, few Germans changed their radio habits. German radio was full of triumphant reports—even as the Wehrmacht was put more and more obviously on the defensive, journalists spoke of "adjusting the frontlines" and "planned rear-flank movements." Though hardly free of propaganda, the BBC was a much more reliable news source. In Berlin argot, Goebbels's mendacious radio addresses quickly became known as "Clubfoot's Fairy-Tale Hour."

But even those who saw through Nazi propaganda had to acknowledge the Nazis' expertise in using the media for their own purposes. Besides radio propaganda, the importance of which Hitler had recognized early on, there were weekly newsreels devoted entirely to spreading Nazi ideology. Goebbels's fondness for cinema inspired him to risk an experiment in filmed political humor, and in early years of the war, the Propaganda Minister had comic sketches included in the weekly newsreels. The first such series was called "Tran and Helle" and was based on a simple formula. A stubborn fellow with a shaved head named Tran (played by actor Ludwig Schmitz) would run through litanies of complaints, read books by Jewish authors, or buy oranges on the black market, that is, do everything possible that a good racial comrade would call wrong. Then the dapper party loyalist Helle would bring the "defeatist" back into line. Often Helle's "well-intentioned" bits of advice were laced with threats. This was the case in a sketch about listening to foreign broadcasters:

HELLE: *That's great that you finally bought a radio receiver. Now you'll know what an interesting age we live in. You can follow the major announcements of the empire.*

TRAN: *And maybe I can tune in occasionally to foreign broadcasters.*

HELLE: *What? You want to listen to foreign radio?*

TRAN: *Sure, foreign news. From London, for example.*

HELLE: *London?*

TRAN: *Yeah. Do you know how to get London?*

HELLE: *I don't know how to get London, but I know what you'll get if you succeed.*

TRAN: *And what's that?*

HELLE: *The clink, even prison!*

TRAN: *And if no one finds out?*

HELLE: *It doesn't matter if someone finds out or not. A good German doesn't do things like that.*

TRAN: *But you have to be aware of what's around you.*

HELLE: *Of course, the foreign broadcasts tell the truth pure and unadulterated. Haven't you ever heard about the news system used by our enemies? If you did, you'd know that everything they say is intended to weaken our capacity for resistance.*

Bizarre as it may seem, Germans found the "Tran and Helle" sketches hilarious. But that doesn't mean they agreed with Helle's didactic statements. In fact, more often than not, the opposite was true. Nazi spies reported that the series was so popular because most people sympathized with Tran, the defeatist, whereupon Goebbels immediately canceled it. After the failure of this attempt at humorous persuasion, the fascists never again tried their hand at political sketches—a similar series called "Liese and Miese" was called off in the conceptual stage. Astonishingly enough, after World War II, Jupp Hessels, the actor who had played the Nazi ideologue Helle, claimed he was an apolitical person who never suspected the sketches were anything but harmless entertainment.

DESPITE ALL THEIR propagandistic twisting and turning, the Nazi leadership could not conceal the fact that the war had gone sour. The first hints of a turning tide came during the winter of 1941–42, when the insufficiently equipped Wehrmacht suffered a series of costly defeats in the vast expanses of Russia. In particular, the generation of Germans who had experienced two-front warfare in World War I began to suspect that Hitler had overextended himself in attacking the Soviet Union. But it wasn't just the specter of Verdun that created unease. Many Germans saw a parallel with Napoleon, who had suffered a crushing defeat in wintertime Russia. Moreover, the gigantic, icy Soviet empire was only one of the enemies the German field commanders had to face, and it was becoming evident on other fronts—for example, in Egypt—that the German army had reached the limit of its materiel and personnel. The full might of Göring's Luftwaffe was unable to defend German cities from aerial attack. German cities had been under bombardment since 1940, and by 1943, the Allies were flying bombing missions around the clock. Göring had once famously remarked that if an enemy aircraft ever entered German air space, you could call him Meier. By 1943, wisecrackers among the populace were calling him exactly that, and the notoriously arrogant field marshal had no one but himself to blame.

The course of World War II changed irrevocably with the bloody defeat of German forces in Stalingrad in late January and February of 1943. The demise of the Wehrmacht's Sixth Army permanently disposed of Hitler's boast that he was the "greatest field general in history." Henceforth, the Führer's claims of infallibility would be measured against reality. Hitler himself stubbornly refused to acknowledge the facts and responded to disaster with incessant calls on Germans to persevere. But Hitler was not the only one who grew even more irrational when faced by the ever-widening gap between the true state of affairs and Nazi wishful thinking. The entire National Socialist leadership, now on the defensive, began lashing out. By the time Goebbels made his notorious "total war" speech on February 18, 1943, total war was already a bloody reality on all fronts. In effect, Germany's bloodthirsty aggression was in great part directed against its own army. Tens of thousands of German soldiers were needlessly sacrificed abroad, while on the home front the SS took command.

Outward and inward radicalization proceeded hand in hand. During the intoxicating series of German victories early in the war, the fascist legal system had made only moderate use of measures designed to intimidate skeptics. Now death sentences were handed out fast and furiously to "those who undermine defensive strength." The sentences and executions that followed were based on a nefarious emergency wartime ordinance thought up by Field Marshal Wilhelm Keitel. The text of the ordinance was left purposely vague:

> Undermining defensive strength is punishable by death, and this punishment applies to whosoever publicly calls upon and encourages others to refuse to serve in a German or allied army and otherwise tries to weaken or undermine the will of the German people and their allies to preserve themselves.

Starting in 1943, the Nazi judicial system made liberal use of what amounted to a blank check for arbitrary state violence. Judges were creative in their interpretations about what sort of statements counted as "public," and courts decided that even critical comments made in family circles fell under Keitel's ordinance.

Judges and prosecutors relied on the help of a small army of eager informers who delivered hundreds of fellow citizens critical of the regime to the gallows throughout the remaining years of the war. Sometimes the informer was a building superintendent or a neighbor trying to settle an old score. In extreme cases, children even informed on their parents. Nowhere in German society were people safe from these unofficial Nazi "deputies." Without informers, who were of course encouraged by the state, the regime could have never achieved the level of coercion it did over its own citizenry. The Gestapo itself, although widely feared, lacked the personnel necessary to keep millions of people under its thumb. Instead of beefing up the secret police, the Nazis came up with a perfidious system whereby tips could be passed all the way from nosy neighbors to the highest levels of the Gestapo.

IN HER ANALYSIS of Nazi secret police files, the historian Meike Wöhlert has given us a good picture of what happened to people who were handed over to the Gestapo for telling defeatist jokes. In most cases, they were interrogated and then released. Further consequences were rare. Even in those cases where individuals were sent up before special political courts, the trials usually ended with mere warnings. Jokes did not normally fall under Keitel's emergency wartime ordinance, but rather were subject to a far milder law concerning malicious remarks. The small minority of wits who were remanded to "protective custody" were typically released after five months in prison. Nazi authorities treated political criticism—"defeatist remarks"—as a felony and political humor as a misdemeanor.

Nonetheless there were a few exceptional cases in which the telling of jokes was seriously prosecuted in order to get rid "racial comrades" who had fallen out of favor. One of these cases, from the final years of the war, merits further attention: that of the Viennese actor Fritz Muliar. This committed Nazi detractor had been drafted in 1940 and sent to fight in France. When his fellow soldiers learned of his theatrical background, he was ordered to stage an evening of entertainment for the troops. This was hardly unusual. Other performing artists were assigned this task, which was aimed at maintaining morale, and a number of comedians who had successful careers after the war had performed in army cabarets. It was expected that such people would provide apolitical, unchallenging humor that would distract soldiers from the everyday hardships of war. From the beginning, however, Muliar refused to adhere to this unwritten rule. Controversial humor, as Muliar recalled in an interview for this book, went down well:

> "Whenever I told jokes that didn't precisely toe to the party line, there was lots of laughter. And of course, that made me more and more audacious… A master sergeant, an Austrian named Müller, once warned me to be a bit more cautious because things could change in a hurry."

Muliar refused to take that advice. His work in occupied France brought him into contact with French locals who had no love for their conquerors. According to one French joke, the Nazi Party acronym NSDAP stood for "Nous sommes des Allemands provisoires" ("we are the provisional Germans"), and the jokes told by such "provisional Germans" were cutting, anti-German and full of resentment. Muliar was always ready to assist the French, helping them smuggle refugees across the border and supporting other subversive activities. He also retold French jokes among German troops.

An Austrian comrade, a high school teacher from Vienna's first district, reported him to the authorities. A short time later, while standing watch over a fake airfield full of prop airplanes, Muliar was arrested. He was imprisoned in Auxerre and charged with violating Paragraph 5 of the emergency wartime ordinance. Specifically, he was accused of undermining troop morale with defeatist utterances and jokes. And indeed, the young soldier had hardly been circumspect, publicly remarking, "Goebbels is a whoremonger, Hitler a criminal, and the war a lost cause."

It was an open secret that the officers in Muliar's unit were just as blunt in their humor, but they could get away with it. Muliar had already attracted the disapproving attention of party authorities because of his contact with the French and his membership in an Austrian nationalist movement. The jokes he had told made a handy excuse to put the young rebel on ice. Muliar was sent into solitary confinement for seven months, during which time his situation remained torturously uncertain. When he was let out, to stand trial by the military court of the 10th Luftwaffe division, the judge was surprisingly lenient, having apparently concluded that Muliar's remarks did not reflect any deep-seated political convictions but were instead an expression of youthful rowdiness. He was given a four-month prison term for "undermining defensive strength" in addition to a further four-month sentence for an act of theft he had not committed.

But the relief Muliar felt was short-lived. As soon as he arrived back in prison in Auxerre, his case was reopened. The highest military judge in the division, General Field Marshal Huge Sperrle, had found Muliar's sentence far too mild. Muliar was told he would be retried and that the prosecution would ask for the death penalty. After receiving the news, the 22-year-old sat down in his cell and composed his last will and testament. Part of that will was a heartbreaking letter to his family, accompanied by instructions that his gold watch and his copy of Goethe's *Faust* be given to his friend Kurt Jelinek.

On December 12, 1942, Muliar's long wait came to an end when he was taken to Paris and forced to appear in front of a military court. And once again he was spared, sentenced to "only" five years in a reeducation prison. This term was later commuted to "frontline parole." He was sent to the Donets Basin in Ukraine, where he had to serve in a division for military prisoners that was little better than a suicide commando. Miraculously, Muliar survived the war, despite being forced to advance through minefields. He himself figured he was a goner. Decades after the war, he recalled, "Back then I believed I was never going to be able to laugh again."

SERVING IN A suicide squad on the Eastern front was no doubt hellish, but at least Muliar lived to tell the tale. A certain Marianne Elise K., who worked as a technical draftswoman in Berlin, was not so lucky. A colleague in the armaments factory where she worked reported her to the authorities for telling the following joke:

Hitler and Göring are standing atop the Berlin radio tower. Hitler says he wants to do something to put a smile on Berliners' faces. So Göring says: "Why don't you jump?"

Marianne K. was hauled up in front of the notorious People's Court, which had for some time been making a hated name for itself by handing out harsh sentences. The court's president, Roland Freisler, who more than anyone else personified Nazi state judicial terror, sat in person over her trial. The judgment he rendered on June 26, 1943 read:

> As the widow of a fallen German soldier, Marianne K. tried to undermine our will to manly defense and dedicated labor in the armaments sector toward victory by making malicious remarks about the Führer and the German people and by uttering the wish that we should lose the war. By these actions and the fact that she claims to be Czech when she is in fact German, she has excluded herself from the racial community. Her honor has been permanently destroyed and therefore she will be punished with death.

Marianne was executed by guillotine. The court rejected her defense that she was bitter about the fact that her husband had fallen in a senseless war of aggression. On the contrary, the court found that her status as a war widow aggravated her crimes.

The People's Court made it a point of pride to take no account of individual suffering. Freisler's predecessor, Otto Georg Thierack, had given the incoming president clear instructions:

> *In general, the judges of the People's Court must accustom themselves to seeing the ideas and intent of the state leadership as primary and the human destinies that depend on them as secondary.*

Freisler embraced these words and enforced what they enjoined to the letter. As the war progressed, the number of cases heard and of death sentences handed out by Thierack and Freisler's court rose dramatically. In 1942, the year in which it became clear that the fortunes of war would turn against Germany, the death toll increased tenfold.

Year	Death sentences
1937	32
1938	17
1939	36
1940	53
1941	102
1942	1192
1943	1662
1944	2079

"Defeatists" like Marianne K. were almost invariably executed, and the court did not distinguish between everyday citizens and people who were well known. One of the court's victims was the internationally renowned pianist Karlrobert Kreiten, who was summoned before a judge after prophesying that the Nazi government would soon have one head fewer. Even the personal intervention of world-famous conductor Wilhelm Furtwängler, director of the Berlin Philharmonic Orchestra, could not avert Kreiten's fate. The announcement of the pianist's execution was celebrated in a Berlin daily newspaper with a sarcastic editorial bearing the headline "Artist—Example and Role Model." The author of that article was a journalist named Werner Höfer, who despite his Nazi past would go on to make a career in West German television in the 1960s. He was even allowed to host a popular morning TV show and serve as a programming director.

Another prominent "defeatist" was the actor Robert Dorsay, who had achieved fame playing a charming ladies' man in a number of UFA comedies. Along with his acting abilities, Dorsay was very skilled at telling jokes—something he did on every possible occasion. It was his wont to make fun of Hitler and Goebbels at glamorous UFA parties, and not all of his jokes were harmless. One played on the German idiom "to bite into grass," meaning to push up daisies:

> At a procession of the Führer through a city, young girls line the streets carrying flowers. One of them hands Hitler a bunch of grass. "What am I supposed to do with this?" Hitler asks. "Eat it," the girl answers. "People are always saying that better times will only come when the Führer bites into grass."

Dorsay doesn't seem to have considered that not everyone would find such jokes funny. He ignored a couple of judicious warnings and explicitly refused to join the Nazi Party. It was clear to everyone: Dorsay had no time for the Nazis.

In return he was systematically punished. UFA bosses saw to it that he was not given any more major roles. In the anti-Semitic comedy *Robert and Bertram*, he appeared fleetingly as a Jewish servant who could have been a caricature from *Der Stürmer*—a sign of how far his star had fallen. But even this halfhearted attempt to curry favor by sinking to the most primitive anti-Semitic depths could not slow his professional demise. During the war, Dorsay was forced to accept poorly paid engagements as a frontline cabaret performer, and even the worst film roles were beyond his grasp. Despondent, he vented his frustrations over beer and wine in the commissary of one of Berlin's leading theaters. One day, Dorsay was amusing his table with the latest Führer jokes, and promptly got reported to the authorities by a government counselor who happened to be in the room. In August 1943, a special military court sentenced him to two years' reeducation incarceration. But as Dorsay was preparing to serve that sentence, his case was still making waves.

By the summer of 1943, the state was frantically trying make people show solidarity by adopting ever more brutal punitive measures for skeptics. Heinrich Himmler, who had just been appointed Minister of the Interior, canceled all the sentences handed out by special courts—he apparently viewed them as too lenient. On October 8, Dorsay was retried, and the verdict this time around was death. Less than three weeks later, the actor was executed by guillotine.

The *Völkischer Beobachter* and other Nazi-run newspapers laconically passed on the news of his execution:

Treason punished by death: Berlin, November 1, 1943. The actor Robert Stampa a.k.a. Dorsay was sentenced to death for recurrent agitation against the Reich and for severely undermining our defensive strength. The sentence has already been carried out.

In the next-to-last year of the war, Robert Dorsay's name could once more found on posters. Not film posters, but blood-red announcements on advertising kiosks, put there to ensure that everyone knew how the popular wisecracker had met his end.

THE CASE OF Robert Dorsay once again illustrates the double

standards that were applied in the Third Reich to critical political jokes. Some joke tellers got off with a warning, while others were sent to prison or, in extreme cases, put to death. The reason for the inconsistency, as Wöhlert has shown, was not the arbitrary nature of Nazi legal verdicts. The judges were acting systematically on orders that emphasized the defendant's attitude over his actions. Someone like Dorsay, who was known as a critic of the regime, could expect a much harsher sentence if brought up before a court than a committed National Socialist who told the same joke. This guiding principle of the Nazi judicial system can be traced back to an order from Hitler himself, as passed on by Heydrich in 1936.

The draconian punishments handed down by the People's Court were aimed at making examples of certain individuals and could hardly have failed to have at least part of their desired effect. As the number of death sentences increased, so did people's feeling of being under threat when they told jokes critical of the regime. Yet this does not mean, as has been so often suggested, that laughter in the Third Reich was deadly. Merely telling a political joke did not put the joke teller's life at risk. The real risk arose when the Nazis were looking for an excuse to remove an unwanted member of the community. What mattered was not the "misdemeanor" itself, but the overall picture the authorities made of a defendant's attitude toward National Socialism. A good example is a joke that appeared in a number of official protocols:

Two pictures, one of Hitler and one of Göring, are hanging on the wall of a school with a space left in the middle. A teacher asks, "What should we use to fill the gap?" A pupil stands up and says, "A picture of Jesus. The Bible says he was nailed up between two criminals."

A Gestapo and special-court file from 1933 refers to the telling of this joke as a misdemeanor. But when a priest critical of the Nazis told a variation of the joke in the final years of the war, the People's Court, which had assumed responsibility for the case, handed down a death sentence. The irony was that in the priest's version the meaning of the joke had been concealed so that only those with a firm knowledge of the Bible could grasp it:

> A mortally wounded soldier is about to die and calls a nurse. He says, "I'm going to die as a soldier and I'd like to know for whom I've given my life." The nurse answers: "You are dying for the Führer and the German people." The soldier asks, "Can the Führer come to my bedside?" The nurse says: "No, that's not possible, but I'll bring you a picture of him." The soldier tells her to put it on the right-hand side of his bed and then says, "I was in the Luftwaffe." So the nurse brings him a picture of Göring and puts it to the left of the bed. Then the soldier says, "Now I can die like Jesus."

What led to the death sentence was not the content of the joke, but the biography of the priest who told it.

Joseph Müller was a Catholic, born in 1884 and raised by deeply conservative and religious parents. Like many other young men of his generation, he volunteered for the German army in World War I and returned home wounded and traumatized, after fighting in France and Romania. He studied theology in Freiburg and Münster and was appointed a priest in 1922. He immediately showed an aptitude for youth work and by the 1930s was giving as many as 17 hours of religious instruction a week. The melancholy, at times depressive clergyman blossomed whenever he had the opportunity to win over young people for the church. Politics were part of what he taught, and he often warned his pupils against chasing after "spectres," that is, extreme political positions.

This inevitably brought on conflict with the local Nazi faithful, who preferred to see their children in the Hitler Youth and the German Girls' Association, rather than in Sunday school. Besides, over time Müller opened his house and yard not just to children but also to Polish forced laborers. Ostensibly, they were there to do gardening work, but this was just a pretense so that they could take part in the Mass. That violated the law, as did his public "defeatist" insistence that Germany would never be able to win the war.

Although he had never been officially in trouble with the authorities, Müller no longer had a clean record in Nazi eyes. He began his last assignment near the city of Hildesheim on August 1, 1943, with a number of secret black marks against him. Müller probably would not have known how precarious his situation was. His friends described him as naïve, and his immediate superior reported that he was only moderately intelligent and lacked "intellectual flexibility." Nonetheless, he quickly made friends in his new home, and decades later people still praised his kindness. He did not realize that a local carpenter who often carried out repairs in his rectory was a fanatical Nazi.

About a month after his arrival, Müller had a conversation with a local schoolteacher, and the teacher told him the joke about the dying soldier. He had heard it in a pub, where it reportedly elicited hearty laughter from a group of farmers present. On his way home, Müller accidentally bumped into the carpenter and his father, who was feeling ill. To cheer up the old man, and possible as a bit of revenge on the carpenter, who often made cracks about religion, Müller told the joke he had just heard. The carpenter proceeded immediately to the local Nazi group leader and denounced the priest.

It was the stone that signaled an avalanche. The denunciation was passed on to the Hildesheim Gestapo, and secret police officers appeared at one of Müller's services and began demonstratively taking notes. The priest was hauled in for interrogation. Afterward, he was released, because the Hildesheim Gestapo was waiting for instructions from the Main Reich Security Office in Berlin, which had also taken an interest in the case. The machinery of state injustice, the perfidious system that depended on informers like the young carpenter, sputtered into action. Critical clergymen had been atop the Nazis' black list for a number of years, and in 1942 another priest who had worked in the bishopric of Hildesheim had been murdered in the "priests' block" of the Dachau concentration camp.

Over the next three months, Müller was repeatedly summoned for Gestapo interrogation. During those interviews, he repeatedly stressed that he never intended to make a joke at the Führer's expense, but rather had seen the story of the dying soldier as a parable of Christian willingness to sacrifice that might have cheered up the carpenter's father. He maintained this ineffective line of defense in the months that followed, steadfastly refusing to reveal the name of the person who had told him the joke. Meanwhile, the People's Court had gotten involved in the investigation and was insisting that the "defeatist" be arrested. By that time, the carpenter regretted what he had done and had secretly met with Müller in a neighboring village. The carpenter recanted his statement and asked that the investigations be halted, but without success. Müller was arrested in his rectory on May 11, 1944.

Witnesses reported that the police entered the house through the back door to prevent Müller from fleeing. At first, he was held in Hildesheim, but after a few days, the authorities, claiming that they had to treat him for acute stomach pains, transferred him to a prison in the Moabit district of Berlin. On July 15, he was presented with the charges he would face at the People's Court. His trial for "undermining defensive strength" commenced three weeks later, only a few days after the failure of another attempt to assassinate Hitler, this one led by Count Claus Schenk von Stauffenberg. The defendant could hardly have faced the court at a more inauspicious time. Four courageous members of Müller's parish who had offered to testify on his behalf were refused admittance to the court.

The trial, over which Roland Freisler himself presided, quickly turned into a travesty. Freisler repeatedly interrupted Müller's attempt at a defense in order to berate the priest. Müller's brother Oskar would later report that the judge even interjected religious jokes during cross-examination:

Freisler manipulated the testimony as he pleased. It needs to be recorded that during the cross-examination of witnesses Freisler could not resist making cutting, cynical jokes and hostile remarks against Christianity, the Pope, Catholic bishops, and priests. This turned directly blasphemous, when a witness related a joke that mocked the Christian belief in heaven and hell, as Freisler himself helped the witness find words of common scorn. The method of recording evidence also made it clear that the Nazis had kept the priest under observation because they feared that his work—what they meant was his restless zeal among parish youth—would have undone everything the party had built up there.

Oskar Müller's report suggests what was really being tried was not the transgression Müller was accused of committing, but rather a belief system that contradicted National Socialism.

Even in the middle of his wildest outbursts, Freisler was able to argue coherently. As court protocols reveal, his worst ravings were still articulate. He was also a keen observer, and by the time of Müller's trial he must at least have suspected that Germany would be defeated in World War II. By 1944, that much was obvious to every clear-thinking person. But Freisler allowed his rationality to be overridden by an almost religious faith in the Führer's promises of final victory. Anyone who challenged this faith shook the tenuous foundations of Freisler's entire belief system. By the penultimate year of the war, the gulf between reality and Nazi wishful thinking was such that it took significant mental exertion to bring the two together. For Freisler, representatives of Christianity were nothing less than heretics who threatened him with an alternative to National Socialism.

That was likely the reason for the judge's hysterical pedantry and scornful tirades against "Bible huggers." Müller's trial was not really about a joke or the "defeatist" utterance of an individual. It was about mounting a desperate defense of an extreme and therefore vulnerable position, namely, that in the end, through sheer force of will, National Socialism would defeat every enemy. Amid the signs of general social disintegration that had commenced with the latest failed assassination attempt against Hitler, the death penalty was the only outcome Freisler could entertain for the Müller trial. Only the shedding of blood, so the judge reasoned in his verdict, could repair the sickness in the "inner front." As was so often was the case with the trials Freisler heard, the Müller proceedings concluded with an orgy of yelling. Oskar Müller wrote:

What followed was one of Freisler's enraged outbursts, in which he pelted the defendant with all sorts of accusations of collusion, hostility, and destructive intention toward National Socialism in the midst of a war for survival. Like a worm, Freisler raged, the defendant had bored his way into the marrow of the German people and undermined its will to self-defense. There was only one way to expiate such a sin: the death penalty.

At 1 p.m. on September 11, 1944, Müller was taken to the guillotine and beheaded—and as usual in Nazi Germany, every minute detail of the execution followed an exact protocol.

A bill for the costs of the execution was sent to Müller's heirs, who were forbidden from holding any sort of memorial service. In the last town where Müller had served, the owner of a pub was given the "friendly warning" that she could be the next to face capital punishment, since there was too much talk about the priest in her establishment. Even in the final months before the demise of the Third Reich, the state apparatus of repression remained fully functional. But Roland Freisler would only survive Joseph Müller by a few months. Nazi Germany's most notorious hanging judge was killed in an air raid in early February 1945.

BY 1944, Germany had irrevocably lost the war. Even the commander of German forces on the Western front, Field Marshal Gerd von Rundstedt, admitted in September of that year that the Nazi empire's military collapse was a mere matter of time. After the Allied landing in Normandy on June 6, there was no holding back the enemy, and by August 25, American and French resistance troops had liberated Paris. The Allied army was growing in number and achieved victory after victory. In particular the Third Army, under General Patton, was quickly gaining ground and pressing forward from Metz in Alsace to the Mosel River in Germany. In August, the Seventh Army under General Patch had landed on France's Mediterranean coast and was speeding its way up the Rhone. Meanwhile, the British-Canadian First Army under Field Marshal Montgomery had liberated Brussels and Antwerp. These Allied forces with their gigantic columns of tanks were advancing sometimes as much as 50 miles a day.

The Wehrmacht could do little to slow down their enemies, and the Führer senselessly squandered what resources the German military had left. Instead of countering the advances of Allied troops with flexible maneuvers, Hitler simply ordered the Wehrmacht to dig in and hold out, just as he had ordered them to do at Stalingrad. Contrary to all military logic, key locations were held so long that German units there were surrounded and fell to attrition. Such human losses didn't concern the Führer. He was working on a fantastical plan for a counterattack that would ultimately seal the destruction of his army.

Elsewhere in the theater of war, on the periphery of the hopelessly overstretched Nazi Empire, the situation was even graver. Despite the much heralded deployment of General Rommel, the so-called Desert Fox, to Northern Africa, that region fell to the British. Hitler probably never fully comprehended the strategic significance of this loss. The populace saw the situation more clearly and began referring to "Tunisgrad," harking back to the Stalingrad fiasco. The worst situation, though, was on the Eastern front, where a gigantic Soviet force was massing. The Red Army's Summer Offensive, about which hand-wringing German generals had warned Hitler, swept across Eastern Europe. By August, vanguard Russian units had worn down the German Army Group

Center, seized the crucial oil fields of Romania, and reached the border of Eastern Prussia.

Within a matter of weeks, the war had reached German soil and could not be beaten back, so Goebbels's propaganda machine tried a new method of bolstering public morale. Rumors were strategically sown throughout the press that German scientists were working on a "miracle weapon" that would turn the tide of the war at the last minute. There was a bit of truth to this. By June 1944, the V1 "flying bomb" was complete, and in September, the V2—the world's first liquid oxygen–powered ballistic missile—followed. Both represented significant technological breakthroughs, but they were not nearly effective enough to have a noticeable impact on the balance of power in late World War II. The V1 usually missed its targets and was so slow that it could be easily intercepted by British warplanes. The V2 could fly at four times the speed of sound but consumed enormous resources and usually buried itself on impact and thus inflicted less than the intended damage. Some 10,000 forced laborers had worked themselves to death in an underground concentration camp, Dora Mittelbau, to produce the infernal weapons, which were developed by physicist Werner von Braun. One of the awful ironies of the German missile program was that more people died making V2 rockets than were ever killed by them.

It is unclear how many Germans believed the fairy tale about a "miracle weapon." Some surely did, since with every German military defeat, people clutched at any straws of hope or comfort. But there was also an indeterminate number of "defeatists" who didn't share the faith. The popular imagination recast the V in the rockets' names, which stood for "retaliation," as the initial for "retardation," "desperation," and even "failure." Jokes circulated about other, even newer miracle weapons, such as the V3, which could fly 4,000 kilometers and bring back prisoners; the V4, a hundred-man tank with four people inside and 96 to push it from behind; and the V5, a massive white flag that Germans were to wave when Allied troops came into sight.

A more militarily significant miracle weapon was the XXI submarine, which could remain submerged for up to 100 hours at a time. These vessels could indeed have inflicted serious damage on the Allies—if they hadn't entered mass production far too late to affect the course of the war at sea. In the end, the story of German submarines in World War II remained one of catastrophes, human losses, and floating coffins. Once again, there was no bridging the gap between propaganda and reality. This became the fodder for a joke that was recorded in a number of variations:

Have you heard that the Navy has a new miracle weapon?—No. What is it?—A two-man submarine with 1.4 meter-thick walls of rubber.—To protect it against being detected by sonar?—No. It will cruise around the coast of England and erase the island.

Most ordinary Germans were more concerned with sheer survival than with Goebbels's propagandistic chimeras. Germany had been under aerial bombardment since 1940. Film clips from 1942 may have depicted Berlin as happy city, but in reality the German capital was slowly but surely being transformed into a heap of rubble. People joked that Rommel would soon be appointed Berlin's Nazi district leader since he was so effective in the desert.

Likewise, once contemporary witness recalled walking by Berlin's heavily damaged Sportpalast auditorium and hearing a schoolmate call out: "Look, they've burned down Bumleg's stage."

Bumleg was a hardly complimentary nickname people had given the clubfooted Goebbels, who had urged the German people to commit themselves to "total war" in a 1943 speech delivered in the Sportpalast.

Berlin suffered hugely as the full force of the war reached Germany. Göring's Luftwaffe was in tatters and could offer little protection against Allied air raids, which involved as many as 1,000 warplanes. Göring had always boasted that no enemy aircraft would ever reach German air space, and this was one of the few things the German masses ever truly held against the portly air force commander. Toward the end of the war, as popular humor turned increasingly black, the following joke was recorded in Berlin:

> *The Nazis' rule is over, the verdicts have been spoken, and Hitler, Göring, and Goebbels are hanging from the gallows. Göring turns to Goebbels one last time and croaks: "I told you everything would be decided in the air."*

In general, jokes about the Nazi political leadership became more and more insulting. One popular joke, variations of which were recorded in Vienna, Cologne, and Berlin, was aimed straight at the Führer:

> *Hitler and his chauffeur are driving through the country, when there's a crash. They've run over a chicken. Hitler says to his chauffeur: "I'll tell the farmer. I'm the Führer. He'll understand." Two minutes later, Hitler comes up rubbing his behind from where the farmer kicked him in the ass. The two men drive on, and a short time later there's another crash. This time they've run over a pig. Hitler tells*

his chauffeur: "You go in this time." The chauffeur obeys,
but it's an hour before he comes out of the farmer's house,
and when he does, he's drunk and is carrying a basket full
of sausages and other gifts. Hitler can't believe his eyes.
"What did you tell the farmer?" he asks. The chauffeur says:
"Nothing special. I just said, 'Heil Hitler, the swine is dead.'"

By the end of the war, Hitler had been brought down to earth. The fictional farmer was not the only one for whom he was no longer the pseudo-divine Führer, but a swine.

Still, the majority of Germans continued to believe the enemy leaders were those in London, Moscow, and Washington. Night after night, hour after hour, gigantic squadrons of Allied bombers flew waves of attacks on German cities. The Luftwaffe having proved so inadequate, local leaders in Berlin and Hamburg built huge citadels with radar-guarded anti-aircraft guns to shoot down enemy planes. That prompted one unknown wisecracker to compose new lyrics for a well-known soldier's song:

On the roof of the world
There's an anti-aircraft unit
They shoot the whole night through
But they never hit shit.

Popular civilian songs were also parodied. One of them was "Es geht alles vorüber, es geht alles vorbei," a big hit for German chanson singer Lale Andersen in 1942. The original lyrics were:

Everything will pass
Everything will be through
But two people in love
Will always stay true.

Lucy Mannheim, a German Jew who had emigrated to London, sang a revised version of the song for the German-language program of the BBC:

> *Everything will pass*
> *Everything will be through*
> *First goes Adolf Hitler*
> *Then the party goes, too.*

> *Every year a December*
> *Is followed by a May*
> *First Adolf Hitler will leave*
> *Then his henchmen will go away.*

The anti-Nazi version of the song became an underground hit in Germany, and various verses were sometimes recited without melody as a poem or a joke—instances were recorded in a number of secret police and Gestapo files. Mannheim's propaganda song was easy to remember and clever, so that it may well have been the most effective product of the BBC German-language satire division.

Nonetheless, in 1944, nothing was over just yet. Along with the sound of Allied bombers, there was the incessant drone of Goebbels's propaganda with its fantasies of "retaliation." The "retaliation" for the Allied destruction of German cities, however, mainly consisted of sacrificing the rest of the Wehrmacht in a senseless offensive in France. The German army was so decimated by that point that on September 25, 1944, Hitler was forced to call up a "Volkssturm," or "popular offensive." This consisted of Hitler Youth members and of men up to sixty who had previously been deemed unfit for military service but who now received a crash course in the use of anti-tank weaponry. This pathetic militia didn't stand a chance against the well-trained, well-equipped soldiers of the Red Army and Western Allies. By the end of the war, 170,000 Volkssturmers were reported missing, most having presumably been killed.

This inspired a macabre take on a popular German nursery rhyme:

Fly away, June bug,
Your father's gone to war
And they'll draft your grandpa too
For retaliation here,
Fly away, June bug!

Other jokes were equally bleak. In one, a man who's digging around in a cemetery with a spade is asked if he's recruiting new members for the Volkssturm. In another, even that option is exhausted:

What has gold in its mouth, silver in its hair, and lead in its
bones? A member of the Volkssturm.

Another joke proposed that the Volkssturm was in fact the long-awaited miracle weapon, since when the Russians caught sight of Germany's new fighting force, they'd all die laughing.

No doubt the sight of pensioners ("late-vintage Hitler Youth" was another crack) and teenagers in uniform inspired pity among civilians. People remarked ironically that soon those born in 1943 would be rolled out to the front in their baby carriages, or that Hindenburg had applied for a leave of absence from Saint Peter to join the men of his year, who had also been called up. Despite the rough tone of these jokes, they were born of desperation, and not scorn for the unfortunate cannon fodder.

There were other signs as well that told the civilian populace that the end of the war was at hand. Fearing a repeat of the shortages and starvation of World War I, Hitler had always seen to it that Germans had enough eat. This was done in the interests of maintaining morale on the home front and not out of actual concern for people's welfare, but whatever the reason, German-occupied territories were ruthlessly plundered to keep Germans well fed. People in Poland and Ukraine in particular suffered under these measures. But as the war progressed, and Germany yielded more and more of this territory and bombing campaigns cut off supply routes, the food situation worsened. German civilians may not have suffered anywhere near as much as people in occupied countries, but they were still forced to tighten their belts.

Considerable popular ire was directed at the shortages, while most Germans studiously ignored the fact that huge stretches of conquered territory had been bled dry to keep Germany suitably nourished. In Vienna, residents approached rationing with their typical caustic humor:

Hitler calls a meeting with Göring, Goebbels, and Food Minister Herbert Backe. Hitler says to Göring: "How long will our planes and fuel last?" "Five years, my Führer," Göring answers. Hitler turns to Goebbels: "How long can your propaganda keep the people in line?" "Ten years, my Führer," Goebbels answers. Hitler then turns to Backe: "And how long can you kept us fed?" "Twenty years, my Führer," Backe says. Hitler is delighted. "Then we can keep waging war for a long time yet," he says, whereupon Backe timidly raises his hand. "Um, I only meant the four of us."

The Allies' strategy of wearing down the German people's will with constant aerial bombardments hadn't worked, but the populace was now afraid their enemies would starve them to death. Another joke played both on worries about food and the sandbags with which people tried to barricade themselves during air raids.

> *Churchill takes a reconnaissance flight over Germany. When he returns, he sighs: "There's no use trying to starve out the Germans. They've hoarded so many provisions, the sacks are coming out their cellar windows."*

Night after night, the civilian population, which by that point basically consisted of women, children, and invalids, would seek the safety of cellars. In the early days of the air raids, warning sirens would sound a half hour in advance of an attack, but in the final months of the Third Reich, people were lucky if they got a few minutes' notice. Anyone who couldn't get to a bunker or a cellar was left alone, defenseless, to face carpet-bombing.

An anonymous diary writer described the mood and the humor of those who sought refuge in the flickering emergency light of German cellars in the final days of the Third Reich:

> 10 p.m., in the basement. After my evening soup, I lay on my bed for a while and then proceeded on down. The entire cellar community was already there. There was little shooting today, and although it's about the hour for it, there's been no bombing. People are nervously cheerful and begin to tell stories. Mrs. W. exclaims: "Better a Russian on your belly than an American on your head." The joke doesn't fit well with the mourning she's wearing.

Frau Behn crawls through the cellar, "Let's be honest, shall we? None of us are virgins anymore."

At the end of the war, eastern Germany was subject to more than bombardment. The Russian "miracle weapons" were also approaching—batteries of primitive rocket launchers that the Germans called "Stalin organs" for their high-pitched yowling whine. These devices were anything but precise, but they could fire up to 54 rockets simultaneously, and their effect was devastating. Residents of Berlin came up with morbid names for city districts and locations, such as "Rubblefield," "Rag Palace" and "Bomb Crater West," that reflected the devastation. People greeted one another on the street with "Have a shrapnel-free night," or "Stay well and tend my grave."

In the final months of the war, reality was like a film being played in fast motion. Hitler's last-gasp Western offensive failed pathetically after a month, and the last act was drawing near. The Red Army overran the coal-rich region of Silesia, prompting Armaments Minister Albert Speer to remark dryly to Hitler, "The war is lost." On April 9, 1945, the East Prussian city of Königsberg (Kaliningrad), which Goebbels once called a fortress, capitulated after suffering near total destruction. Two weeks later, the battle for the German capital was raging. The Red Army had to take the city arduously, street by street. In Vienna, too, German resistance was fierce—people fought for every house in the district of Simmering. But despite all these efforts, Hitler's Germanic state was growing smaller by the day.

The populace took the last developments of the Third Reich with gallows humor:

One guy says to another, "Tell me, what are you going to do after the war?"—"I'm finally going to take a vacation and see all of Germany."—"And what are you going to do in the afternoon?"

Another question people began asking, in the face of obvious inevitable defeat, was what would become of Hitler. That gave rise to the following joke, alluding to Hitler's habit of saluting by raising but not extending his right hand.

Why does Hitler have such a funny way of doing the Hitler greeting? After the war, he wants to become a waiter.

On April 30, 1945, all speculation was over. The Russians had fought their way to the Imperial Chancellery, and there, hidden four stories underground, Hitler shot himself in the head.

No jokes about Hitler's suicide have survived. No matter how much his pseudo-divine aura suffered in his final months, the populace was shocked by the Führer's death. With an incomprehensible, almost childish faith, many Germans had continued to worship their leader until the very end. No one seems to have felt in the mood to make any funny remarks.

Heinz Rühmann in *The Gas Man* (1939)

Ludwig Schmitz and Jupp Hessels in a "Tran and Helle" skit

To Be or Not To Be, 1942

A break on the set during the filming of *The Great Dictator*, 1940

Fritz Muliar, around 1941

Frankreich 31. Oktober 1942.

Mein letzter Wille!

The 22-year-old Muliar's last will and testament

sollte uns etwas zustoßen so sind zu verständigen, respektiere sie den Herren?
zu übergeben:

Was ich besitze gehört meiner Mutter Frau L. Müller Wien VII/62 Kanndlg. 1
Meinem Freund Kurt Nachmann Wien II. Zirkusgasse 10, vermache ich meinen
Gold-Ring mit dem Onyx. Es soll ihm Glück bringen.
Meinem Freund Kurt Jelinek (Wien) vermache ich zu treuen Händen meine
kleine Gold-Uhr. Er hat diese seinem Sohn Jürgen an dessen 10. Geburtstag
zu übergeben.
Frau Gretl Heinz-Schröter, sie erhält die Proustausgabe von Hutter. Des
Faust aus meiner Sammlung.

Zu benachrichtigen und zu grüßen sind:
Frau Friedl Hofmann-Feldmann Wien III. Theresianumgasse 6
Frl. Maria Kieslich Wien IV. Joh. Straußg. 37.
Herr Alfred Epstein Wien VII Neubaug. 80
Familie Donig Wien II. Meiner Cousine Hilde ist ein Andenken zu übergeben.
Herr Leo Förster u. Herr Felix Bernard beide Wien.
Herr Dr. Peter Hehle Wien III. Am Heumarkt 9.

Aus meinem Gold-Siegelring soll ich meine Mutter ein Kreuz machen
lassen und dieses als Anhänger tragen.

Ich wünsche beerdigt zu werden, nach Möglichkeit in Wien im Grabe
unserer Familie am Zentralfriedhof.

Mein letzter Wille.

Nur von meiner Mutter Frau L. Müller Wien VII/62
Kanndlgasse 16/1 zu öffnen.

Jm Namen
des Deutschen Volkes

In der Strafsache gegen

die technische Zeichnerin <u>Marianne Elise K</u> ███████████████ geb.
Tomandl aus Berlin-Mariendorf, geboren am 1o. August 1921 in Elster-
berg (Vogtland),

zur Zeit in dieser Sache in Untersuchungshaft,

hat der Volksgerichtshof, 1. Senat, auf Grund der Hauptverhandlung
vom 26. Juni 1943, an welcher teilgenommen haben

als Richter:

Präsident des Volksgerichtshofs Dr. Freisler, Vorsitzer,
Landgerichtsdirektor Stier,
ℋ-Standartenführer von Dolega-Kozierowski,
Generalarbeitsführer Voigt,
Ortsgruppenleiter Kelch,

als Vertreter des Oberreichsanwalts:

Erster Staatsanwalt Ranke,

für Recht erkannt:

Frau Marianne K ███████████████ hat als deutsche Krieger
witwe unseren Willen zu mannhafter Wehr und tüchtiger Arbeit für den
Sieg in einem Rüstungsbetrieb durch gehässige Worte über den Führer
und das deutsche Volk und den Wunsch, wir möchten den Krieg verliere
zu untergraben gesucht.

Sie hat sich so und dadurch, daß sie sich als Tschechin
aufführte, obgleich sie doch Deutsche ist, außerhalb unserer Volks-
gemeinschaft gestellt, ihre Ehre für immer verwirkt und wird deshalb
mit

dem T o d e

bestraft.

The announcement of the death sentence handed down to Marianne K.

Joseph Müller, circa 1943, and a list of the charges leveled
against him in the People's Court

aufgestellt. Dieser sagt darauf: Jetzt sterbe ich wie
Christus!!! (Hier deckt sich der Wortlaut nicht mit dem Pro-
tokoll der Gestapo, wo steht ... zwischen zwei Verbrechern)

In diesem Augenblick wurde N. von seiner Ehefrau an den
im Obergeschoß des Hauses aufgestellten Fernsprecher gerufen
und mußte sich deshalb entfernen. Er nahm an, daß der A.
durch seine Erzählung hatte zum Ausdruck bringen wollen,
wie einst Christus zwischen zwei Schächern gestorben sei,
so habe hier der Soldat zwischen zwei Verbrechern sein Leben
enden müssen. Darüber, daß der Führer und Reichsmarschall in
dieser Weise von dem A. als Verbrecher bezeichnet wurde,
war N. auf das tiefste empört. In der Überzeugung, daß der
A. eine Gefahr für den Nationalsozialismus sei, wandte er
sich an den stellvertretenden Ortsgruppenleiter der NSDAP,
den Molkereibesitzer Rierk, bat diesen, zunächst mit niemandem
darüber das, was er ihm mitteilen würde, zu sprechen, und
teilte ihm dann das von dem A. Gehörte mit, um mit ihm zu
besprechen, was gegen den Angeschuldigten zu unternehmen sei.
Rierk erklärte jedoch, daß sie derartiges nicht für sich be-
halten dürften und erstattete gegen den A. Anzeige.

III.

Bl.7/8.   Der Ang. hat zugegeben, bei den beiden von N. geschilder-
ten Gelegenheiten mit diesem zusammengetroffen zu sein. Nach
seiner Darstellung hat er im Übrigen N. erklärt, niemand
könne sagen, ob der Krieg von Deutschland gewonnen werden
würde, oder ob er etwa so wie der erste Weltkrieg enden würde.
Die Lage sei ernst. Es würde ihm bitterweh tun, wenn die
Jugend aus dem jetzigen Kriege ebenso heimkehren müsse, wie
er selbst aus dem ersten Weltkriege. - Der Bolschewismus
würde sich aber von den schweren Schlägen, die er erhalten
habe, nicht erholen können, sondern verblute sich. - Der
Nationalsozialismus sei vom historischen Standpunkt aus be-
trachtet durch die Arbeitslosigkeit, die Inflation und das
Versagen der anderen politischen Systeme zur Macht gelangt. -
Bei seiner Unterhaltung mit N. hat er, auch davon gesprochen,
daß sich Ostarbeiter im Reich in Arbeit befänden. Er habe
aber daran keine abfällige Kritik geübt. In seiner Erzählung
von dem sterbenden Soldaten habe er lediglich den Tod des
Soldaten mit dem Tode Christi vergleichen und darlegen wollen
daß der Soldat wie Christus in Erfüllung einer Aufgabe für
eine Idee stürbe.

XI.

Ein bezeichnendes Gerichtsdokument

Abschrift: Gerichtskasse Moabit 13099/44.   A n s c h r i f t

An die Erben des Joseph Müller
z. Hd. von Herrn Pfarrer M ü l l e r
in A c h t u m , Post Hildesheim.

Stempel der
Gerichtskasse
in Moabit

Reichsanwaltschaft beim Volksgerichtshof — Staatsanwaltschaft.
Geschäftsnummer 5 J 170/44.

Kostenrechnung
in der Strafsache gegen Joseph M ü l l e r
wegen Wehrkraftzersetzung.

Lfd. Nr.	Gegenstand des Kostensatzes und Hinweis auf die angewandte Vorschrift	Wert des Gegenstandes	Es sind zu zahlen	
			RM	Pfg
1	2	3	4	
	Gebühr für die Todesstrafe .		300	—
	Postgebühren		—	24
	Zeugen- u. Sachverständigen-			
	gebühren		63	50
	Transportkosten		31	—
	Haftkosten			
	a) für die Haft vom 12. Mai			
	1944 bis 11. September 1944			
	= 123 Tage à 1,50 RM . .		184	50
	Porto		—	12
			579	36
	Von der Strafanstalt werden			
	eingehen		131	—
			448	36

Absender: Berlin NW 40.   den 10. Oktober 1944.
Turmstraße 91.   Kassenstunden von 9 bis 13 Uhr
Fernsprecher 35 67 01.

Gerichtskasse Moabit
Postscheckkonto Berlin 34 564

Kassenzeichen:
13099/44.

134

The bill sent to Müller's family for his execution

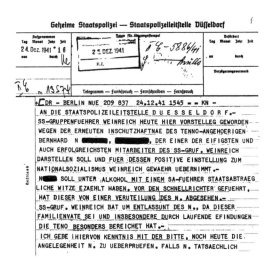

+CDR - BERLIN NUE 209 837 24.12.41 1545 - - KN -
AN DIE STAATSPOLIZEILEITSTELLE D U E S S E L D O R F.-
SS-GRUPPENFUEHRER WEINREICH HEUTE HIER VORSTELLG GEWORDEN - -
WEGEN DER ERNEUTEN INSCHUTZHAFTNAE DES TENNO-ANGEHOERIGEN
BERNHARD N ████, ████████, DER EINER DER EIFIGSTEN UND
AUCH ERFOLGREICHSTEN MITARBEITER DES SS-GRUF. WEINREICH
DARSTELLEN SOLL UND FUER DESSEN POSITIVE EINSTELLUNG ZUM
NATIONALSOZIALISMUS WEINREICH GEWAEHR UEBERNIMMT .-
N███ SOLL UNTER ALKOHOL MIT EINEM SA-FUEHRER STAATSABTRAEG
LICHE WITZE EZAEHLT HABEN, VOR DEM SCHNELLRICHTER GEFUEHRT,
HAT DIESER VON EINER VERUTEILUNG DES N. ABGESEHEN.-
SS-GRUF. WEINREICH BAT UM ENTLASSUNT DES N., DA DIESER
FAMILIENVATE SEI UND INSBESONDERE DURCH LAUFENDE EFINDUNGEN
DIE TENO BESONDERS BEREICHET HAT.-
ICH GEBE IHIERVON KENNTNIS MIT DER BITTE, NOCH HEUTE DIE
ANGELEGENHEIT N. ZU UEBERPRUEFEN. FALLS N. TATSAECHLICH

LEDIGLICH WEGEN DES WITZEERZAEHLENS ERNEUT IN SCHUTZHAFT
GENOMMEN WORDEN SEIN SOLLTE, BIN ICH IM HINBLICK AUF DIE
HERANSTEHENDEN FEIETAGE MIT EINER UNTERBECHUNG DER SCHUTZHAFT
BIS ZUM JANUAR EINVERSTANDEN.-

REICHSSICHERHEITSHAUPTAMT - M U E L L E R, SS-GRUPPENFUEHRER.+

Dauerdienst   Düsseldorf, am 24.12.1941

1. Fernschreiben:
                    An die Aussehdienststelle
                    in W u pper t a l

Einsetzen von [bis]aus vorstehendem FS.
Dann fortfahren: Von dem Veranlassten bitte ich mir Mit-
teilung zu machen.   Stapoleit.Düsseldorf
                                - Dauerdienst -

2. Zum Vorgang.
                                Im Auftrage:

                                Krim. Ass.

A mild verdict passed against someone who told an anti-Nazi joke

The actor Robert Dorsay and the announcement of
his execution, addressed to his wife

Gericht der Wehrmacht-
kommandantur Berlin

Abteilung X
Berlin-Charlottenburg 5
Witzlebenstr. 4-10

Bln.-Charlottenburg 5, den 30.10.43
Witzlebenstr. 4-10
Fernruf: 30 06 81

17

St.L. X Nr. 2020/43a

Frau
   Louise Stampa-Dorsay

   B e r l i n W 62
   Lutherstr. 21
   Pension Hemmann

Anl.: 1 Brief

   Das am 8.10.43 ergangene Todesurteil ist nach
Bestätigung am 29.10.43 vollstreckt worden.
   Todesanzeigen oder Nachrufe in Zeitungen,
Zeitschriften und dergl. sind verboten.
   Ausgefertigt   I.A.
                                gez. Dr. Haas
   Heeresjustizinspektor   Kriegsgerichtsrat

VI. HUMOR AND ANNIHILATION

THE DARKEST CHAPTER of the Third Reich began in the shadow of the all-consuming war in Eastern Europe. Hitler implemented a brutal policy of "freeing" the German people from groups of human beings he considered "vermin" and "parasites" and charged his best organizer, Heinrich Himmler, with carrying out this murderous task. The SS leader was given the title Imperial Commissioner for the Reinforcement of Germanity, and his assignment was to put Hitler's idea of creating additional living space for Germans in Eastern Europe into practice in the occupied countries. The plan was to resettle Germans on the broad plains of Ukraine and Russia, where they were to farm the land like their Germanic ancestors. The populations who presently lived there were to be driven into exile or enslaved.

As for Jews who lived in Germany and Eastern Europe, the Nazis devised an infernal "final solution" to their presence. The technical details were planned at the Wannsee Conference in January 1942. The full settlement endeavor—"General Plan East"—was only to commence after the war; for now, the extermination of European Jews was given top priority. With astonishing criminal energy, Himmler and his henchmen perfected their techniques for murder. Every time the Wehrmacht advanced into new territory, a wave of thugs followed, ready to carry out pogroms and mass executions.

As strange and as tasteless as it might seem today, these anti-Semitic orgies were the subject of jokes at the time. The tellers, however, were not uninvolved Germans or those carrying out the murders, but the Jews themselves, who used humor to try to keep up a brave front in the face of impending catastrophe. Even the most hopeless situations lost some of their ability to terrify, if one laughed at them. Astonishingly, a number of these jokes were preserved by people who survived the Holocaust. Austrian-French author Manés Sperber recorded the following drastic, deeply tragic example:

> A Jewish village in Eastern Europe has been victimized by the most horrific sorts of attacks, pogroms, and mass shootings. One of the villagers escapes to the neighboring town and tells everyone what's going on. He's asked: "And what did you do?" He answers: "Last time, we recited all 150 psalms instead of the usual 75. And we fasted on the Day of Atonement." "Good work," came the answer. "You can't just sit around doing nothing."

This joke reflects widely held belief that Jews let themselves to be led like lambs to the slaughter. But the punch line isn't really critical of them. The naiveté and innocence of the Jews in the joke throws the bloodthirsty crimes committed by the world around them into sharper contrast.

The compilations of Jewish jokes by writer Salcia Landmann contain examples based on the mass shootings carried out by the Nazis in Eastern Europe:

> The Gestapo is about to shoot some Jews when the commanding officer walks up to one of them and growls, "You almost look Aryan, so I'll give you a chance. I wear a glass eye, but it's not easy to tell. If you can guess which eye it

*is, I'll let you go." Immediately, the Jew answered, "The left
one!" "How did you know?" asks the Gestapo commander.
"It looks so human."*

While "action units" were carrying out mass liquidations on the
eastern front, the SS was feverishly at work on the next stage of
their annihilatory program. Hitler was not content to kill only the
Jews of Eastern Europe—he wanted to eradicate Jews throughout
all of Europe. Per an ordinance of September 1, 1941, all persons of
"Jewish blood," regardless of whether they were German, Dutch,
or French, had wear a yellow Star of David in public. The idea was
to give Jews a visible stigma that made it easier to exclude them
from the rest of the community.

Those required to wear the star were essentially forced to run
the gauntlet every time they stepped into the streets of their home-
towns. Still, many Jews reacted to the daily insults with humor.
French Jews, for instance, quickly dubbed the star the "pour le
Semite" ("only for Jews"), as if it were a badge of honor. But the ordeal of discrimination was nothing compared to the fear of being
deported to the east. The Nazis cynically called the deportations,
which commenced in early 1941, "resettlements" and "transfers of
residence." None of those resettled, though, ever came home.

In Germany, people studiously kept silent about the disappearance of their former neighbors, although nobody believed
the myth that they had been sent east to some special, paradisia-
cal Jewish village. Jews themselves were of course painfully aware
of what was really happening, as the following joke shows:

*How many types of Jews are there? Two: optimists and pes-
simists. All the pessimists are in exile, and the optimists are
in concentration camps.*

It's possible that nobody understood exactly how horrific the Jews' situation in Eastern Europe was and that few comprehended the hellish dimensions of the system Himmler and Eichmann were constructing. But it was obvious to all that deportation was a journey with no return. Conditions in German concentration camps had been deteriorating ever since the beginning of the war. In 1939 there were no highly organized mass exterminations, but thousands died in the camps from malnutrition and disease. Those who were detained there existed in dire and inhumane circumstances.

Food rations were also unfairly distributed in Nazi-occupied territories, and those unlucky enough to be classified as Jews were hit hardest. The historical record has preserved the following backhanded compliment:

Our occupiers know a lot about nutrition. They've scientifically determined that Germans need 2,500 calories a day to survive, while Poles require only 600 and Jews just 150.

An even bitterer joke was recorded in occupied Amsterdam, where a number of Jews simply starved to death after German occupiers deliberately gave them insufficient food rations:

A guy wanted to commit suicide and tried hanging himself. But the quality of the rope in the noose is so bad it breaks. So he tried sticking his head in the oven, but they shut off the gas between two and five in the afternoon. Then he tried living on his rations. That worked like a charm.

If they had the means, Jews paid horrendous sums on the black market for additional food. It was senseless to save the money, since anyone could be deported at any time, and many people suspected that where they were going in Eastern Europe, money wouldn't do them any good. It was better to exchange every cent for necessities.

Starving the Jews was of course just one element in the Nazis' horrific plans. The screws in the deadly machinery of the final solution were constantly being tightened, and there was no escape. Among the Nazis' victims, there was a feeling of increasing hopelessness, since with the start of World War II routes into exile had been closed off. That desperation clearly resonates in the following joke:

> *The Nazis take over Austria, and a Viennese Jew goes to a travel agency to inquire about the possibility of emigrating. The agent takes out a globe and points at various countries. "Emigration to Palestine is forbidden, the American quota is already used up, it's hard to get a visa for England, you need financial guarantees for China, Paraguay, and Brazil, and Poland won't even let Polish Jews back in." So the Jew says, "Don't you have another globe?"*

Jews crammed into the overcrowded ghettos were entirely at the mercy of their Nazi tormentors. All potential paths to freedom were blocked, and only the lucky few managed to evade the long arm of the Nazi state and the ever more frequent orgies of anti-Semitic violence. Some succeeded in procuring false identification or going underground.

But very few Gentile fellow citizens offered Jews any real help. Most often, the entreaties of those who were trying to flee state murder fell on deaf ears. This, too, was reflected in a joke, playing off the rationing of wine:

A Jew asks a friend from his school days to take him in. When the friend timidly admits he is too afraid, the Jew takes his leave, giving his friend a bottle of wine. "What's this for?" asks the friend. "That's so you can later say in good conscience that you had an Oppenheimer concealed in your basement."

Jews who were captured while hiding out underground were put into the next cattle car heading east. Some were taken to preliminary holding camps; others were sent straight to extermination factories like Auschwitz, where SS men decided on the train station platform who would live and who would die. As many as 10,000 people were gassed to death at Auschwitz every day.

Despite Nazi attempts to conceal the gruesome murder camps, the German public could hardly have been shielded completely from mass killings of this scope. Not every German was aware of Nazi extermination policies; most didn't want to know the truth. Most Germans were like the Three Wise Monkeys from Japanese legend, covering their ears, eyes, and mouth so as to block the truth. Many people did not want to acknowledge the crimes against humanity that were being committed in the name of Germany and the moral abyss in which they plunged all Germans. But the smoke continued to issue from the crematorium chimneys, not just in Eastern Europe but also near a number of small German towns, and it was impossible to prevent some information about the Holocaust getting through to the general public.

Jews in Amsterdam seem to have known about the gas chambers. That is suggested by the following joke, which refers to Abraham Asscher and David Cohen, the two heads of the Jewish Council in the occupied Dutch capital, who were often accused of collaborating with the Nazis:

*Asscher and Cohen are summoned to Nazi headquarters
and told that the Jews are to be gassed. Asscher immediately asks, "Are you going to deliver the gas, or do you want
us to take care of it?"*

This sort of extremely black humor was not all that rare. Coco
Schumann, a German-Jewish jazz musician who survived Auschwitz, later recalled that even Jews in concentration camps told
jokes in an attempt to cheer themselves up. That testimony is
backed up by letters written by a Jew from Amsterdam in the
holding camp Westerbork.

SOME SIX MILLION Jews were murdered during the Third
Reich, a number that represents six million individual stories.
One was the story of Fritz Grünbaum, who had been interned
in various concentration camps since the Nazi takeover of Austria. Grünbaum was particularly unlucky because of his physi-
cal appearance. He was slight of build and had the sort of face
that called to mind anti-Semitic stereotypes, making him an ideal
object for Austrian Nazis' racist hatred. They wasted no time in
arresting the clever, self-effacing comedian and sending him to
Dachau in Germany. He would never see his wife again—they
would be reunited only in death.

Grünbaum, who was in his mid-fifties, was forced to do hard
labor in the camp, but he never lost his sense of humor, and he
performed cabaret routines in his scant free time to cheer up himself and his fellow inmates. The other prisoners showered him
with applause and small gifts. In September 1938, though, he was
transferred to Buchenwald, where he was held in even more se-
vere conditions. He managed to survive the food shortages of the

first wartime winter, but he had the misfortune to be recognized by one of the guards, who knew him from his Austrian cabaret days. From then on, Grünbaum had to make the SS men laugh on command or face a beating—a sadistic punishment if there ever was one. His fellow prisoners conspired to shield him from work in the stone quarries, which he would scarcely have survived. Instead, he was assigned to repair socks in a knitting factory. But that job did not last; the camp commandant decreed that knitting was too easy a job for Jews. The SS made him clean latrines, as part of what they called Column 4711. The guards showed "pity" only once: after they tormented Grünbaum's colleague Paul Morgan to death, they allowed Grünbaum and chanson singer Hermann Leopoldi to bring their friend's body to the gates of the camp.

No amount of coercion can completely rob a born comedian of his sense of fun. About the systematic undernourishment of inmates, Grünbaum used to joke that not eating was the perfect cure for diabetes. But his flippant gallows humor could not conceal the fact that Grünbaum was growing progressively weaker. In October 1940, he was transferred back to Dachau; by that point, he was already suffering from tuberculosis of the stomach and intestines. He gave his final performance behind barbed wire, telling a couple of coarse jokes and singing some of his most famous couplets. After that appearance, an eyewitness reported, he collapsed from exhaustion. A few days later, he unsuccessfully tried to commit suicide. On January 14, 1941, the star comedian died. The coroner's report cynically registered the cause of death as "coronary paralysis."

That same year, the fortunes of the German comedian-director Kurt Gerron also began to change for the worse. Up until 1937, Gerron had been able to make films while in exile in the Netherlands, and he was also responsible for the Dutch-dubbed version of Disney's *Snow White and the Seven Dwarfs*. He had built a new life for himself away from his home country and proved he was capable of surviving. But in 1940 Holland was conquered by Nazi Germany, and the occupiers began ratcheting up the pressure against Jews and political enemies. Gerron was already on the Nazis' blacklist. Regarded by the fascists as a stereotypical Semite, he had made an involuntary guest appearance in the notorious Nazi movie *The Eternal Jew*, whose director had simply appropriated footage from another film in which Gerron had acted. A voice-over explained to viewers how this footage demonstrated that "film Jews" such as Gerron loved to play dubious characters in hopes of achieving a comic effect. The German Office of Public Information ordered that this instructive film be screened in all Dutch cinemas. *The Eternal Jew* would be the last time that Gerron would be seen in a film in wide release.

Gerron's stage career was also drawing to a close. Together with his friend Otto Wallburg, who lived in the same Amsterdam boarding house, Gerron had performed in a number of émigré cabaret evenings. Under German occupation, Jewish comedians and actors were only allowed to appear in the Joodsche Schouwburg, a theater in the city center, which had been known as the Hollandse Schouwburg before the German invasion. Now the Nazis wanted to see the stage used for shows by and for Jews. The neoclassical building on the Plantage Midenlaan would soon achieve tragic fame, when it was used as an assembly point for deportations. In 1943, after the theater had been closed, Gerron, too, would end up back there—the very place where he had once given acting lessons. From there he was taken to the Westerbork holding camp on the Dutch-German border. The trains leaving Westerbork headed east, most directly to the gas chambers of Auschwitz.

While interned at Westerbork, Gerron ran into two old acquaintances, emcee Willy Rosen and comedian Max Ehrlich. On orders from the camp commandant, who fancied himself a minor patron of the arts, the three men were forced to form a cabaret trio. Their first show, *Da Capo!*, was performed for an audience comprised partly of inmates and partly of guards. The Westerbork cabaret became a somewhat ghoulish institution. Former inmates recalled that performances were always scheduled one day in advance of deportations. We will never know whether the commandant, Konrad Gemmecker, came up with this arrangement out of pure sadism or whether he truly wanted to distract the prisoners from their impending doom. Gemmecker, however, was not known for kindheartedness.

In 1944, Gerron was once again crammed into a cattle car. He would never see Germany again. He was taken to the Terezin (Theresienstadt) ghetto in what is now the Czech Republic. His reputation as a filmmaker and actor had spared him a direct trip to Auschwitz. Famous prisoners were often given a short stay of execution before they were shipped off to the extermination camps. Gerron had also, as was noted in his file, served Germany honorably in World War I, which was perhaps another reason why he was not immediately sent to be gassed.

The place where Gerron spent his final days bears a horrific historical legacy. In peacetime, this former outpost of the Austrian Empire had been a sleepy garrison town, but the Nazis converted it into a concentration camp. There Reinhard Heydrich, Himmler's nefarious deputy, had built a model ghetto for Jews forcibly moved from there from other parts of Europe. The "ghetto" was a trick to convince foreign observers that the Nazis were treating Jews well. Theresienstadt was a false front behind which the Final Solution could proceed undisturbed. In order to ensure that commissions of foreign observers left with a positive impression, Heydrich's henchmen made all sorts of calculated "improvements." To temporarily alleviate the chronic overcrowding, the SS would deport large numbers of Jews to Auschwitz before commission visits. Cafés were hastily set up on camp grounds, and the commandant ordered prisoners to stage operas. The aim was to create the impression that Jews had it better than many frontline soldiers.

Among those fooled by such cheap tricks were a contingent of Red Cross observers sent at the behest of Danish government. As always happened, the minute these delegates departed, the cafés and theaters were dismantled. The reality of Theresienstadt had nothing whatever to do with coffeehouse charm. Concentration camp life was terrible, inhumane, and potentially deadly. Only a small minority of the approximately 144,000 inmates survived their mistreatment at the hands of the SS. Epidemics took a heavy toll, and the prisoners were chronically undernourished. In the year 1942 alone, 16,000 inmates died of starvation and illness. By the time Gerron entered this "waiting room for hell," thousands more people had been sent from it to certain death in Auschwitz.

Gerron's reputation preceded him, and soon after his arrival the former UFA director founded a new cabaret in Theresienstadt—on the orders of the commandant, an SS man named Karl Rahm. A temple of popular entertainment fit in perfectly with the cynical plans of the SS, that is, using the camp to keep up appearances. Gerron named his cabaret The Carousel, suggesting the gaudy fun of a merry-go-round. Yet the terrible truth was that in Theresienstadt only one merry-go-round turned mercilessly; it flung those on the Nazi's death lists straight to Auschwitz.

Despite his constant fear of being deported there himself, Gerron went about his new task calmly and methodically. There was no shortage of suitable performers for the theater in the Jewish model ghetto. The crème de la crème of the Jewish theater and art scene were interned in the former garrison—from star composers to top-rated emcees, glamorous chanson singers, and acrobatic artists. The Carousel has been described as the premier German-language cabaret of the 1940s. Nor was Gerron averse to taking the stage himself. But the Golden Twenties were long gone. The comedian, who had once starred in the stage version of *The Blue Angel*, was now playing only to emaciated inmates in prison stripes, watched over by brutal SS men wearing their death's-head insignia.

On one occasion, the troupe was ordered to perform in a space in which dozens of naked corpses had been piled up. The players were horrified, but the performance was not canceled. Since the actors shied away from the dead bodies, Gerron summoned the camp's blind inmates and had them form a human chain. Protected by their disability from the sight of their gruesome burdens, they passed the corpses from hand to hand, out of the hall and down the stairs, where a man with a wheelbarrow took them away. The show went on that very evening. This grotesque dance of death in the middle of death's way station made a bizarre prelude to the acts that evening; a paradigm of the thoroughly schizophrenic attempt to elicit laughter in a place of immeasurable horror. Gerron, who had nothing left to lose, devoted himself to his productions with all the energy at his disposal.

GERRON'S SHOWS were so successful that in the summer of 1944 the SS made him a new offer. For the first time in four years, he would once again take his seat as a film director. The title of the project was *Theresienstadt: A Documentary Film from the Jewish Settlement Region.* The idea for the film came from SS leader Hans Günther and was given a budget of 35,000 marks. Every last cent of it had been confiscated from Jews—an ironic detail much to the taste of the Nazis who had conceived this movie, an especially perfidious piece of propaganda. The film would depict the concentration camp as a utopia, a kind of sanitarium for Jewish "guests." Once more, the deception was aimed at foreign observers, especially those from neutral countries. The script included scenes to be shot in Theresienstadt's nonexistent cafés and nightlife boulevards. Shots of a hospital and other social amenities were also planned. Naturally, the pseudodocumentary would not mention that inmates were being sent in droves to Auschwitz.

Gerron became an involuntary Nazi collaborator, and carried out his enforced task with his usual thoroughness and energy. In fact, he had little choice. In one scene from the film, Gerron himself appeared in front of the camera, performing together with a music duo and comedy trio on an open-air variety stage outside the ghetto walls. Gerron's last performance as a cabaret artist, committed to celluloid that day, has been lost—the film survived only as a 20-minute collection of fragments. It gained international attention after the war under the title *The Führer Gives the Jews a City.* It's unclear how the film got this cynical title, since it was not released by the SS. Most probably it was named by the inmates themselves. Coco Schumann, who survived both Theresienstadt and Auschwitz, recalls that camp prisoners were constantly telling jokes, each more blackly humorous than the last. So the idea that they could have come up with the outrageous title is not implausible.

The backstory of the Theresienstadt documentary ended, as things always did in the nightmarish world run by Himmler, in a tragedy. One by one, the actors who had pretended in front of the camera that they lived in a paradise were deported to Auschwitz and murdered. In late October 1944, it was Gerron's turn. Some witnesses reported that the comedian-director bore what was essentially a death sentence with pride and stoicism. Others say he fell to his knees and begged a guard to spare him before the cattle cars rolled out. Whatever the case may have been, he was taken from Theresienstadt to Auschwitz on October 28, 1944, and sent to the gas chambers immediately upon his arrival. He was murdered together with his seriously ill colleague Otto Wallburg, whom the Nazis had captured in occupied Holland. On October 30, two days after these two great stars of the Weimar Republic met their pitiful, horrific end, the final solution program in Auschwitz was permanently suspended.

Gerron's last film was completed by Czech cameraman Karel Peceny and edited by Peceny's countryman Ivan Fric. The fake documentary has rarely been screened in public. In any case, it never fooled anyone. By the latter days of World War II, before the film was ever shown, the Nazis' crimes against humanity had already become known to the foreign public.

VII. LAUGHING AT AUSCHWITZ? HUMOR AND NATIONAL SOCIALISM AFTER WORLD WAR II

IN THE IMMEDIATE aftermath of World War II, hunger and chaos ruled Germany. The former "master race" was fighting for sheer survival, and most people weren't concerned about what had taken place in the past. Time passed, and Germany was divided, with the West experiencing the "economic miracle" of the 1950s and East concentrating on making "actually existing socialism" a reality. West Germans didn't want to remember, and East Germans were freed of any responsibility for doing so, since the official line of the Communist state was that fascism had been a Western phenomenon. Perhaps that was why the postwar period—the late '40s and early '50s—produced few new political jokes in either the West or the East.

There were, however, as Auschwitz survivor Ruth Kluger relates, a number of jokes in questionable taste about Jews returning to Germany to reclaim property that had been stolen from them. In Vienna, for instance, people would ask, "And has your Jew come back?" Many former citizens of the German Empire had learned nothing from history—not because they were stupid, most likely, but because in order to draw lessons from the past, they would have had to face it squarely, and that they did not want to do. So former hardcore Nazis were able to rise back up through the social ranks in both the West and the East, and the period in general was characterized by an ugly superficiality.

Most Germans wore blinders, and anti-Semitic prejudices were not at all out of place in good society.

It would take a further generation for the situation to change in West Germany. During the 1960s and '70s, Germans began in earnest to investigate and acknowledge the horrors of the past, as the demands of young people overcame the stiff resistance of the war generation. The painful process revealed bottomless abysses, although many older Germans never stopped repeating the mantra that they had known nothing about the Holocaust. In such an emotionally charged situation, it was practically impossible to laugh about Hitler.

As far as mainstream cultural depictions of the Holocaust were concerned, a number of unwritten rules began to crystallize. The American Holocaust scholar Terrence Des Pres summed them up as three conventions:

1. The Holocaust shall be represented, in its totality, as a unique event, as a special case and kingdom of its own, above or below or apart from history.
2. Representations of the Holocaust shall be as accurate and faithful as possible to the facts and conditions of the event, without change or manipulation for any reason—artistic reasons included.
3. The Holocaust shall be approached as a solemn or even sacred event with seriousness admitting no response that might obscure its enormity or dishonor its dead.

There were, of course, breaks with these conventions, but artists who deviated from them experienced varying receptions.

Sometimes, the public granted individual filmmakers and comedians a kind of tacit "license" to make fun of Hitler's regime.

Most postwar German critics, for instance, applauded Chaplin's *Great Dictator*. It was scarcely conceivable that a German reviewer would have dared criticize a figure so iconic in the Anglo-Saxon world as Charlie Chaplin, and it was generally recognized that Chaplin's intentions had been thoroughly noble. Although the film is arguably one of the funniest ever made, it was clearly aimed at drawing attention to dangers of subscribing to Nazi insanity. The German reception of Billy Wilder's 1961 comedy *One, Two, Three,* which featured a whole menagerie of bizarre, heel-clicking pseudo-Nazi figures, was similar.

German critics were always ready to accept anti-Hitler comedies, but the criteria by which they judged them changed over the years. The more time passed, the more relaxed Germans became about depictions of the Führer as a ridiculous tin-pot dictator. To reflect that change, cultural historians Kathy Laster and Heinz Steinert added two new rules to Des Pres's three conventions:

4. The province for depictions of the Holocaust is "high culture." Popular cultural productions are automatically considered suspect and more superficial. Comedies appeal mostly to an audience that isn't necessarily well educated. Therefore, it's more difficult for comedies to be taken seriously as high culture.
5. The artist needs to have the correct attitude and motivation: altruism, good intentions, the proper moral and didactic aims. Even when a piece of culture is comic, the artist has to display appropriate seriousness.

But by the end of the 1960s, the American comedian-director Mel Brooks would break all the rules—written and unwritten—of historical piety.

A scene from Mel Brooks's *The Producers* (1968)

A scene from *La Vita e Bella* (1997)

Adolf, the Nazi Sow, depicting a pint-sized Hitler
and a transvestite Göring

The Holocaust may not have been the focus of Brooks's 1968 film *The Producers*, but the part it played in the story was anything but politically correct. Two Broadway producers conspire to defraud their investors. To cover up their criminal undertaking, they intentionally plan a massive flop, reasoning that no one is going to bother to check the books of a show that was a box-office disaster. In order to guarantee that their production is a failure, they hire a notorious neo-Nazi to compose a musical, and when the deranged fellow, in all seriousness, delivers a script entitled *Springtime for Hitler,* the producers think they have come up with the perfect scam. But they are drastically mistaken. The show, in which female Nazis cavort on stage in lingerie, becomes a huge comic hit. The producers' scam is uncovered, and the two are sent to jail.

There is no hint of "appropriate seriousness" in Brooks's blockbuster, and the film never pretends to be high culture. But audiences loved the impious, unconventional idea, and Brooks was justifiably rewarded with an Oscar for best screenplay. "If you stand on a soapbox and trade rhetoric with a dictator, you never win," Brooks would remark years later in a magazine interview. "But if you ridicule them, bring them down with laughter, they can't win. You show how crazy they are." German critics, without exception, agreed—not least because the director was American and Jewish. A similar German production might have been given a far rockier reception. The discomfort many Germans felt with ridiculous depictions of Hitler was hardly a thing of the past in 1968.

Brooks' far less successful 1983 remake of Lubitsch's *To Be or Not To Be* also drew critical praise, but that doesn't mean all Anglophone productions were beyond criticism. In 1990, for example, some Germans were outraged by a British TV show, made for the satellite network Galaxy, in which Hitler was portrayed as a petit bourgeois, suburban twit. The premise of *Heil, Honey, I'm Home*, was that Hitler and Eva Braun survived the war and now live in a provincial settlement of row houses. Hitler is constantly quarreling with his Jewish neighbors, the Goldensteins, and is depicted as a narrow-minded bean counter and incessantly complaining neighborhood pest. The authors used this scenario as a vehicle for all sorts of cheap gags, and even the British press was not amused, complaining that the show trivialized the Holocaust and the suffering of those who had survived Nazi war crimes. Shocked by the reaction, Galaxy pulled the sitcom after only one of eight episodes had been shown. Excerpts from *Heil, Honey, I'm Home* were, however, unearthed for a later show called *The 100 Greatest TV Moments from Hell*.

Such thoroughly negative reviews were hardly a good omen for one of comedy's biggest international stars when he decided to tackle a very touchy subject. In 1997, when Italian comedian Roberto Benigni released *La Vita e Bella* ("Life is Beautiful"), a comedy about the Holocaust, it was hard to imagine a more difficult balancing act. The film begins relatively harmlessly, with a number of scenes introducing the Jewish protagonist, Guido Orefice. With a variety of tricks, and using his overactive imagination, Guido seduces his future wife, Dora, away from a local fascist party secretary. Yet the hero's fantasy life so completely dominates him that he fails to notice the political climate changing around him. He runs away with his bride, for example, on a horse borrowed from his uncle, oblivious to the fact that animal has been painted with Nazi slogans. The second half of the film jumps forward to a time when the bitter reality of fascism has caught up even with this dreamer. Guido and Dora are married and have a son, Giosué. One day, the Germans order that all the

Jews in the village be deported and taken to a concentration camp. Guido, Dora, and Giosué are among these victims. The rest of the film takes place in the camp, which bears a vague resemblance to Auschwitz.

Guido knows that not only is his own life at stake, but also those of his wife and son. To keep the boy calm, Guido tells him that life in the camp is a gigantic game whose goal is to score points—for instance, by hiding himself away during the day while his father is out doing compulsory labor. This deception saves Giosué from the gas chamber. The grand prize for winning the game, Guido tells his son, is a tank, and that prize is "paid out" at the end of the film, when American troops arrive to liberate the camp. But their help comes too late for Guido, who is shot by the SS just before the American soldiers free the prisoners.

The story was challenging, to say the least. Never before had there been a tragicomedy set in a place resembling Auschwitz. Benigni's previous works had been largely harmless comedies. Moreover, he himself was from Italy, a country that had been part of Hitler's Axis. This violated the unwritten rule, recorded by Laster and Steinert, that only Holocaust victims, and not those from later generations, were allowed to engage in this genre of gallows humor. Benigni must have known he was taking a double risk. But the storm of outrage he might reasonably have feared failed to materialize. The few negative reviews the film received were mild, and even critics of Benigni's work conceded that he had adroitly mastered the difficult balancing act. *La Vita e Bella* never seemed exploitative, trivializing, or tasteless. The scant objections that were raised concerned the unrealistic depiction of the concentration camp, and in fact Benigni's setting was no more than a sketch of Auschwitz, with the brutality of the guards and the industrialized murders occurring only on its margins. The

New York Times, for instance, pointed out that life had hardly been so placid in the death camps, and that there had been no children in Auschwitz.

The film's American distributor was nervous and added a written disclaimer, drawing attention to the fictional nature of the plot. But this was unnecessary. It was abundantly clear that *La Vita e Bella* was a kind of fairy tale, and its highly stylized depiction of the Holocaust was one reason the film was so effective. Most people in the audience watched the movie with images of the real Auschwitz in their heads. The first half of the movie, which had all the trappings of a romantic comedy, set up the tragedy of the family's dramatic fall from grace. By the time the three protagonists were deported, the audience thoroughly sympathized with them. There was no need to include the details of historical reality to make viewers appreciate the horrors of that fall, or of the hellish world that replaces Guido's private utopia. Benigni avoided the mistake of switching styles and registers in the middle of the movie. Because the film remained a fairy tale, which made more use of allusion rather than concrete detail, it appealed all the more strongly to the audience's imagination.

Although the hero is killed in the end, *La Vita e Bella* is a film about survival, and the innocent boy Giosué embodies the hope that persists even amid the worst of horrors. Evil is depicted as something ridiculous and banal that will one day pass or be overcome. Even if Guido must die, Giosué survives to grow up in a world without National Socialism. This moral may sound simplistic, but fairy tales are allowed to be dreamy—that is their nature. Benigni won four Oscars in 1997 for his peacemaking, funny and tragic work—a well-deserved recognition for a sensitive take on the Holocaust trauma that never once drifted into triviality.

A year later, German critics were equally mild in their judgment of a far more drastic work of satire by one of Germany's leading comic book artists. Walter Moers' 1998 *Adolf, the Nazi Sow* was another work on the dangerous topic that some initially might have found hard to take. The central premise was that Hitler, complete with center part and moustache, had survived the war hidden in the sewers and reemerged in modern-day Germany. But the old-fashioned dictator is no match for the postmodern world and so becomes embroiled in a series of absurd situations. In one episode, the Führer appears in a popular, real-life TV cooking show, where he explodes in rage in the mistaken belief that the host is Jewish. In another he allows his Tamagotchi to starve, as revenge for what he sees as Japan's betrayal in World War II. "Miserable traitors," the Führer fumes. "Two little atomic bombs, and what do they do? Throw in the towel!" His only consolation is the discovering that his old buddy Hermann Göring also survived World War II and is now working as a transvestite prostitute in Hamburg's red-light district.

Hitler needs all the friends he can get as Moers sends him on a journey through all the clichés of the modern media world, from the cult of Princess Diana to housewives abducted by aliens. Hopelessly befuddled, the ex-dictator is utterly incapable of understanding the country he once ruled and can only vent his frustration in half-articulate outbursts of rage. When he hears the Beatles' "Hey Jude," for example, he's incensed that a song about Jews could be such a hit in Germany. Worse still for Hitler, no one in the brightly colored, comic-book landscape of postmodern Germany pays any attention to the old man's ravings. Modern-day Germany, with its incessant talk-show babble, may be superficial, Moers seems to be saying, but at least there's no place in it for the Führer. Cast adrift in a homeland that has become a foreign country, Hitler can lead nothing more than a shadow existence.

"Real Adolf fans don't find it any funnier than do the anti-fascists," wrote the German newspaper *Junge Freiheit*, which has itself been accused of fascist tendencies, about Moers's work. But in truth, few people in the German media chose to publish their opinions, positive or negative, about the controversial comic. Michel Friedman, then the deputy head of the Council of Jews in Germany and never one to shy away from a fight, merely described Moers's opus as "unsuccessful." Readers were the ones who ultimately judged *Adolf, the Nazi Sow*. With them, Moers's thin volume was a massive hit, selling more than 170,000 copies.

WITH THE PASSING of generations, Germans have become more relaxed about depictions of Hitler as a ridiculous figure. Nowadays, it no longer seems strange for comedians to play the Führer in movies, like Dani Levy's *Mein Führer: The Truly Truest Truth about Adolf Hitler*. What used to be acceptable only for foreign productions is now considered admissible for German works as well. Without the ideological ballast from the past, media outrage at "trivializing" depictions of Hitler seems artificial and overwrought. Temporal distance has done its work. When Germans today watch newsreels from the Third Reich, they are able to see not just the monstrousness of Hitler's regime but also its absurdity. That does nothing to decrease the importance of the Holocaust. On the contrary, people today ask themselves how a generation of Germans could have committed such grave crimes at the behest of a loudmouthed tyrant with a silly moustache. The days of demonizing Hitler are over. Nonetheless, the question of how he could ever have held such power will become harder, and not easier, to answer. For later generations, who have only seen

Hitler in his bizarre appearances in historical newsreels, the appeal of the Führer for the masses is completely mysterious.

Is it permissible to laugh at Hitler? Is a comedy like Mel Brooks's *The Producers* immoral? The respective answers are yes and no. Brooks's film does not decrease the significance of the Holocaust; it reduces Hitler to human dimensions so that people can see him as something other than the evil demon promoted by the historiography of the 1950s. Germans in the Third Reich were neither possessed by an evil spirit nor collectively "hypnotized" by their Führer. They have no claim upon either mitigating circumstance. When we laugh at Hitler, we dismiss the metaphysical, demonic capabilities accorded to him by postwar apologists. All the more pertinent is the question of how the empty trickery of the Nazis, which was already all too well exposed by critics in the late 1920s and 1930s, could have ended in the Holocaust.

On closer examination, the argument, advanced so often in Germany after World War II, that people were unaware of Hitler's demonic maneuvering and were thus more prone to seduction simply does not hold water. The "ridiculous Führer," stripped of his imperial posturing, was by no means a postwar innovation. Enough caricatures exist from the early years of Nazism that depict Hitler as loudmouthed buffoon and tin-pot dictator. The many disrespectful jokes about the Nazi Party leadership that circulated during the Third Reich also support the conclusion that Germans were by no means unwilling victims of propaganda. Great numbers of people back then saw through the swindles cooked up by Goebbels and his gang. Sadly, that did nothing to alter the fact that, in the course of a few years, Germany was thoroughly drawn into the terrible whirlpool of Nazi crimes.

NOTES

I. POLITICAL HUMOR UNDER HITLER

2   "the various collections of 'whispered jokes'"; Among these anthologies, Sellin's should be mentioned in particular since it appeared immediately after the collapse of the Third Reich. The other anthologies of jokes were published with far more temporal distance to their subject matter.

3   "we have no way of knowing precisely how widespread they were."; See Wöhlert, p. 7f.

5   "an expression of Jews' will to survive against all odds."; See Landmann, p. 12.

II. THE RISE AND DEVELOPMENT OF POLITICAL HUMOR

11   "Thus, political jokes could only arise in the modern, secular world."; See Wöhlert, p. 15.

III. THE NAZI SEIZURE OF POWER

32   "...for this reporter nothing special."; See Fest, p. 356.

33   "bellowing out their idiotic favorite song: 'When Jewish blood squirts from the knife, happy days will return.'"; Quoted in Focke/Strocka, p. 15.

36   "This forced entry into the landed nobility earned him the nickname 'von Ribbensnob.'"; See Wiener, p. 85.

41   "They greeted one another with the words 'Swing heil!'"; See Allert, p. 25.

41   "the penalty for noncompliance being the 'slaughter' of the animals."; See Allert, p. 87.

42   "the identity of the true culprit."; See Steinert, p. 264.

43   "I can't imagine anyone believes in Communist culprits instead of a contract job commissioned on behalf of the swastika."; Klemperer, vol. 1, p. 8.

43   "The brothers Sass [SA+SS]."; The Sass brothers were the leaders of a notorious gang of criminals.

49   "a Jewish invention"; Focke/Strocka, p. 143.

54   "Brought into line, brought into line."; Quoted in Kühn, p. 102.

54   "they are one of the many examples of cultural figures declaring their loyalty to the Nazis in those early days."; See Kühn, p. 336.

57   "they have gotten things so obviously wrong."; Hanfstaengl, p. 14f.

58   "he wished to spare the healthy productive masses of the German people from a bloody confrontation with their enemies."; Hanfstaengl, p. 110.

58   "Hanfstaengl's work would 'recall to our minds the heroically pursued struggle of our Führer.'"; Hanfstaengl, p. 32.

59 "His anti-Nazi caricatures had appeared in mass circulation, and Goebbels and his henchmen could hardly be expected to forget his earlier criticisms of fascism."; See E. O. Plauen, p. 43.

62 "Dangerous or not—keep going!"; See Kühn, p. 79.

68 "But the Third Reich did yield a number of instances of precisely that."; Sellin, p. 19.

69 "The harshest sentences for 'maliciousness' were rendered in prewar Nazi Germany"; See Wöhlert, p. 95.

70 "to drag National Socialism and everything holy to National Socialists through the mud."; Finck (2), p. 75.

71 "'Why?' I responded. 'Do I need any?'"; Finck, p. 69.

71 "the 'breeding grounds of Jewish and Marxist propaganda should be closed during their performances and everyone involved, including the audience, should be taken into protective custody.'"; See Kühn, p. 80.

72 "Now that fear is gone. We're already here."; See Kühn, p. 280.

76 "was dragged out of the bed he was sharing with his male lover."; See Fest, p. 636.

77 "formed the basis of a conspiracy not just against the mores of a healthy people but also against the security of the state."; See Wiener, p. 131.

IV. HUMOR AND PERSECUTION

82 "the amount of commerce done afterward by Jewish-owned business did not decline at all."; See Fest, p. 577.

84 "A Jewish great-grandmother. She brought money into the family but not any trouble!"; The legal definition of being Jewish in the Third Reich was having one Jewish grandparent, so people who only had a Jewish great-grandmother among otherwise "Arian" ancestors were not considered Jewish.

87 "None of the other participants made any effort to defend him."; See the interview with Magda Schneider in the 2002 documentary film *Prisoners of Paradise*.

92 "in short she was the heart and soul of the whole theater."; Quoted in Hippen, p. 18.

95 "I, the prince of the land of lies."; Quoted in Hippen, p. 26f.

95 "And we'd have every reason to be ashamed, if we stopped doing that now."; See Hippen, p. 23.

96 "problems of continental Europeans"; See Kühn, p. 55f.

96 "'Escort out' was what the Swiss called the deportations, and in many cases it was an escort to the grave."; See Hippen, p. 14.

97 "an innocent girl whose blood he defiles and thus takes away from her

own people."; See Fest, p. 64.

97   "*Der Stürmer's* readership came up with endless variations on it in the jokes they invented"; See Hanh, p. 225.

102   "Heinrich Hoffmann, whom he repeatedly invited to share evenings of jokes with himself and Goebbels."; See Steinert, p. 327.

103   "Tatzelwurm, the troupe that took over the space previously used by the banned Catacomb."; See Kühn, p. 81.

103   "Churchill a 'drunk'"; See Wiener, p. 37f.

122   "It's not a particularly good Rühmann film, but in war-time, it serves its purpose."; Quoted in Kleinhans, p. 6.

122   "movie entirely in the spirit of my love of flying"; Rühmann, p. 149.

123   "His ability to embody the 'little man on the street' had already made him a star in the Weimar Republic"; The UFA had Rühmann under contract well before the Nazis came to power. This was very unusual at the time for comedians.

126   "no one will doubt that my Semites are genuine."; See Kreimeier, p. 2.

126   "That, in any case, was how the political leadership and their minions in the film industry saw the situation."; Kreimeier, p. 5.

V. HUMOR AND WAR

129   "Only the dumbest calves elect their own slaughterers."; Danimann, p. 58.

133   "Despite having received a few warnings, he was later to write, all seemed quiet on the 'Goebbels front.'"; See Finck, p. 111.

137   "And it's likely that its author was convinced of the propriety of a German attack on Poland."; See Wiener, p. 105.

142   "But in 1940 the vast majority of Germans were intoxicated by Hitler's early military success, and Elser's would long remain the only attempt to assassinate the Führer."; See Shirer, p. 1099.

145   "even the calculating studio bosses began to realize that the United States might not be able to avoid entering World War II."; See Fyne, p. 18.

146   "The story took two years to develop."; Quoted in Schnelle, p. 92.

148   "'Hurry up with your film, everyone is waiting for it.'"; Quoted in Schnelle, p. 95.

151   "Civilizations may crumble—but the hero and heroine come out all right in the end."; Mills, p. 168

152   "Lubitsch, the critic wrote, was a jaded Jewish director."; See Spaich, p. 358.

152   "with many viewers still finding some scenes inappropriate in light of the Nazi genocide in Eastern Europe."; See Fyne, p. 75. This book, which was published in 1994, describes the final scene of *To Be or Not To Be* as "tasteless."

153   "it is certainly a far cry from 'the Berlin born director who finds fun in the bombing of Warsaw.'"; See Spaich, p. 358.

154   "But America in 1942 was not ready for it."; See Spaich, p. 361.

155   "Private on the Western Front"; Lucas, p. 157ff.

158   "No, my racial comrades, I alone am entitled to decide when a year commences and when it concludes."; See Kühn, p. 360.

159   "Whoever intentionally disseminates news from foreign broadcasters of the sort that may endanger the German people's capacity for resistance will be subject to re-educational incarceration and, in extreme cases, death."; *Reichsgesetzblatt* 1, 1939.

163   "Undermining defensive strength is punishable by death..."; §5 of the Ordinance on Special Wartime Criminal Law of August 17, 1938.

164   "The small minority of wits who were remanded to 'protective custody' were typically released after five months in prison."; See Wöhlert, p. 97.

166   "Goebbels is a whoremonger, Hitler a criminal, and the war a lost cause."; Muliar, p. 58.

167   "instructions that his gold watch and his copy of Goethe's Faust be given to his friend Kurt Jelinek."; See Muliar, p. 60f.

168   "Her honor has been permanently destroyed and therefore she will be punished with death."; This comes from the official decision rendered by the People's Court.

168   "Freisler embraced these words and enforced what they enjoined to the letter."; See Koch, p. 217.

169   "Death sentences"; See Koch, p. 222.

170   "Dorsay had no time for the Nazis."; See Liebe, p. 21.

171   "The sentence has already been carried out."; See Liebe, p. 27.

172   "This guiding principle of the Nazi judicial system can be traced back to an order from Hitler himself..."; See Wöhlert, p. 137.

173   "Politics were part of what he taught, and he often warned his pupils against ... extreme political positions."; See Scharf-Wrede, p. 6.

174   "That violated the law, as did his public 'defeatist' insistence that Germany would never be able to win the war."; See Scharf-Wrede, p. 11.

174   "he was only moderately intelligent and lacked 'intellectual flexibility.'"; See Scharf-Wrede, p. 18.

175   "the 'priests' block' of the Dachau concentration camp."; See p. 193 Scharf-Wrede, p. 16.

176   "the Nazis had kept the priest under observation because they feared that his work ... would have undone everything"; See Müller, p. 21.

177   "Freisler allowed his rationality to be overridden by an almost religious faith in the Führer's promises of final victory."; See Koch, p. 231.

178 "There was only one way to expiate such a sin: the death penalty."; See Müller, p. 25.

178 "the Nazi empire's military collapse was a mere matter of time."; See Shirer, p. 1413.

180 "...seized the crucial oil fields of Romania, and reached the border of Eastern Prussia."; See Shirer, p. 1409.

183 "But they never hit shit."; See Wiener, p. 113.

187 "There's no use trying to starve out the Germans... the sacks are coming out their cellar windows."; What was meant were the sandbags used to protect windows from shrapnel.

187 "Let's be honest, shall we? None of us are virgins anymore."; *Anonyma*, p. 28.

188 "The war is lost."; See Shirer, p. 1424.

VI. HUMOR AND ANNIHILATION

210 "thousands died in the camps from malnutrition and disease."; See Kogon, p. 137.

210 "That worked like a charm."; Bolle, p. 103.

213 "Are you going to deliver the gas, or do you want us to take care of it?"; Bolle, p. 144.

213 "That testimony is backed up by letters written by a Jew from Amsterdam in the holding camp Westerbork."; See Bolle, p. 218.

214 "they allowed Grünbaum and chanson singer Hermann Leopoldi to bring their friend's body to the gates of the camp."; See Troller, p. 258.

214 "he was already suffering from tuberculosis of the stomach and intestines."; See Liebe, p. 122.

219 "each more blackly humorous than the last."; See Kluger, p. 62f.

220 "On October 30 ... the final solution program in Auschwitz was permanently suspended."; See Liebe, p. 216.

VII. LAUGHING AT AUSCHWITZ? HUMOR AND NATIONAL SOCIALISM AFTER WORLD WAR II

223 "'And has your Jew come back?'"; See Kluger, p. 62f.

224 "...no response that might obscure its enormity or dishonor its dead."; See Laster/Steinert, p. 184f.

225 "Even when a piece of culture is comic, the artist has to display appropriate seriousness."; See Laster/Steubert, p. 186f.

231 "Benigni must have known he was taking a double risk."; See Laster/Steubert, p. 183.

232 "there had been no children in Auschwitz."; See Laster/Steubert, p. 190.

WORKS CITED

Allert, Tilman: *Der deutsche Gruß—Geschichte einer unheilvollen Geste*, Berlin, 2005 (Eichborn Berlin).

Anonymus: *Eine Frau in Berlin—Tagebuchaufzeichnungen vom 20. April bis 22. Juni 1945*, Frankfurt/ M., 2003 (Eichborn Berlin).

Blasius, Anke: *Der politische Sprachwitz in der DDR*, Hamburg, 2003, in: *Philologia*, Vol.54 (Verlag Dr. Kovac).

Bolle, Mirijam: *"Ich weiss, dieser Brief wird dich nie erreichen"—Tagebuchbriefe aus Amsterdam, Westerbork und Bergen-Belsen*, Berlin, 2005 (Eichborn Berlin).

Broer, Wolfgang: *Wort als Waffe—Politischer Witz und politische Satire in der Republik Österreich (1918–1927)*, Vienna, 1973 (Verlag der wiss. Gesellschaften Österreichs).

Danimann, Franz: *Flüsterwitze und Spottgedichte unterm Hakenkreuz*, Vienna, 2001 (Ephelant Verlag).

Fest, Joachim: *Hitler*, Frankfurt/ M. and Berlin, 1973 (3. ed., 1992; Ullstein-Verlag).

Finck, Werner: *Alter Narr, was nun?*, Munich, 1992 (Herbig-Verlag).

---------------- *Spaßvogel—Vogelfrei*, Berlin, 1991 (Henschel-Verlag).

Focke, Harald and Monika Strocka: *Alltag der Gleichgeschalteten—Wie die Nazis Kirche Kultur, Justiz und Presse braun färbten*, Reinbek bei Hamburg, 1985 (Rowohlt-Verlag).

Fyne, Robert: *The Hollywood Propaganda of World War II*, Metuchen, NJ, 1994 (The Scarecrow Press).

Gamm, Hans-Jochen: *Der Flüsterwitz im Dritten Reich*, Munich, 1963 (revised and expanded ed. 1990; List-Verlag).

Grimmelshausen, Hans Jakob Christoffel von: *Der abentheurliche Simplicissimus teutsch*, Weinheim, 1988 (Reproduction of the first edition from 1668/VCH).

Hahn, Fred: *Lieber Stürmer!—Leserbriefe an das NS-Kampfblatt 1924 bis 1945*, Stuttgart, 1978 (Seewald-Verlag).

Hanfstaengl, Ernst: *Hitler in der Karikatur der Welt*, Berlin, 1933 (Verlag Braune Bücher).

Hartmann, Rudi: *Flüsterwitze aus dem Tausendjährigen Reich*, Munich 1983 (Knaur-Verlag).

Hertling, Viktoria, Wolf Koepke and Jörg Thunecke (eds.): *Hitler im Visier, Literarische Satiren und Karikaturen als Waffe gegen den*

Nationalsozialismus, Wuppertal, 2005 (Arco-Verlag).

Hippen, Reinhard: *Satire gegen Hitler—Kabarett im Exil,* Zürich, 1986 (pendo-Verlag).

Hirche, Kurt: *Der braune und der rote Witz,* Düsseldorf/Vienna, 1964 (Econ-Verlag).

Kleinhans, Bernd: "Propaganda im Film des Dritten Reichs," in: www.shoa.de/filmpropaganda.html

Klemperer, Victor: *Ich will Zeugnis ablegen bis zum letzten. Tagebücher 1933—1945,* ed. by Walter Nowojski, 3rd ed., Berlin 2005 (Aufbau TB).

Kluger, Ruth: *Landscapes of Memory—a Holocaust Girlhood remembered,* London, 2001 (Bloomsbury).

Kogon, Eugen: *Der SS-Staat—Das System der deutschen Konzentrationslager,* Munich, 1974 (Heyne-Verlag).

Koch, Hannsjoachim W.: *Volksgerichtshof—politische Justiz im 3.Reich,* Tübingen, 1988 (Universitas-Verlag).

Körner, Torsten: *Ein guter Freund—Heinz Rühmann,* Berlin, 2001 (Aufbau-Verlag).

Kreimeier, Klaus: "Antisemitismus im nationalsozialistischen Film," in: *Jüdische Figuren in Film und Karikatur,* Stuttgart, 1995 (Jan-Thorbecke-Verlag).

Kühn, Volker: *Deutschlands Erwachen—Kabarett unterm Hakenkreuz 1933–1945,* Berlin, 1989 (Quadriga-Verlag).

Landmann, Salcia: *Jüdische Witze—ausgewählt und eingeleitet von Salcia Landmann,* Munich, 1983 (DTV).

Laster, Kathy and Hanns Steinert: "Eine neue Moral in der Darstellung der Shoah?—Zur Rezeption von, *La Vita e Bella,*" in: *Lachen über Hitler—Auschwitz-Gelächter?,* Frankfurt/ M, 2003 (Edition Text + Kritik), pp. 181–197.

Liebe, Ulrich: *Verehrt, verfolgt, vergessen—Schauspieler als Naziopfer,* Berlin, 1992 (new edition 1995; Quadriga-Verlag).

Lucas, Robert: *Teure Amalie; vielgeliebtes Weib!—Briefe des Gefreiten Hirnschal,* Frankfurt, 1984 (Verein zur Förderung und Erforschung der antifaschistischen Literatur).

Margry, Karel: "Das Konzentrationslager als Idylle: Theresienstadt—Ein Dokumentarfilm aus dem jüdischen Siedlungsgebiet," in: *Auschwitz—Geschichte, Rezeption und Wirkung,* Jahrbuch 1996 zur Geschichte und Wirkung des Holocaust. Frankfurt am Main/New York, 1996, pp. 319–352.

Mills, Robert William: *The American Films of Ernst Lubitsch—A Critical*

History, Ann Arbor, 1976 (Diss. Univ. of Michigan).

Moers, Walter: *Adolf, die Nazi-Sau,* Frankfurt/ M., 1998 (Eichborn).

Muliar, Fritz: *Melde gehorsamst das ja!—Meine Lebensabenteuer,* Graz, 2003 (Steyria).

Müller, Oskar: *Ein Leben in und für Christus—Leben, Wirken, Leiden und Opfertod des Pfarrers Joseph Müller,* Groß Düngen/Celle, 1948 (Eigenverlag).

Plauen, E.O. (Erich Ohser): *Politische Karikaturen, Zeichnungen, Illustrationen und alle Bildgeschichten von Vater und Sohn,* Konstanz, 2000 (Südverlag).

Rühmann, Heinz: *Das war's—Erinnerungen,* Berlin, 1985 (Ullstein-Verlag).

Sauder, Georg: *Die Bücherverbrennung 10.Mai 1933,* Munich, 1983 (Carl-Hanser-Verlag).

Scharf-Wrede, Thomas: *Pfarrer Joseph Müller—Zeuge für Jesus Christus,* Hildesheim 1994 (Sammlung Bistumsarchiv Hildesheim).

Schnelle, Frank: *Charles Chaplins Der Grosse Diktator,* Stuttgart, 1994 (Verlag Robert Fischer + Uwe Wiedleroither).

Sellin, Kurt: *Geflüstertes—die Hitlerei im Volksmund,* Heidelberg, 1946 (Freiheit Verlag).

Shirer, William L.: *The Rise and Fall of the Third Reich,* N.Y., 1950 (new ed., 1992, Random House).

Spaich, Herbert: *Ernst Lubitsch und seine Filme,* Munich, 1992 (Heyne Verlag).

Steinert, Marlies: *Hitler,* Munich, 1994 (Verlag C.H. Beck).

Süß, Wilhelm: *Lachen, Komik und Witz in der Antike,* Zürich, 1969 (Artemis Verlag).

Troller, Georg Stefan: *Das fidele Grab an der Donau—mein Wien 1918–1938,* Düsseldorf/Zürich, 2004 (Artemis & Winkler).

Wiener, Ralph: *Gefährliches Lachen—Schwarzer Humor im Dritten Reich,* Reinbek bei Hamburg, 1994 (Rowohlt-Verlag).

------------ *Als das Lachen Tödlich war,* Rudolstadt, 1988 (Greifen-Verlag).

Wöhlert, Meike: *Der Politische Witz in der NS-Zeit am Beispiel ausgesuchter SD-Bericht und Gestapo-Akten,* Frankfurt, 1997 (Europäischer Verlag der Wissenschaften).

INDEX

PHOTO CREDITS

Photograph of Weiß Ferdl (p. 111), photograph of Karl Valentin (p. 112), photograph of Heinz Rühmann taken from *Der Gasmann* (p. 191), photograph of Ludwig Schmitz and Jupp Hussels as Tran and Helle (p. 192): Courtesy of Filmmuseum Berlin—Deutsche Kinemathek. Photograph of the cast of the Catacomb (p. 110), photograph of Willi Schaefer's Cabaret of Comedians (p. 113), photograph of Werner Finck (p. 109): © Deutsches Kabarettarchiv Mainz. Caricature by E. O. Plauen (p. 107): © Erich Ohser/Peter Ohser. Photograph of Fritz Muliar in uniform (p. 195), Muliar's last will and testament from October 31, 1942 (p. 196–197): © Prof. Fritz Muliar. A still from *La Vita Bella* (p. 227): © Cecchi Gori Group Tiger Cinematografica/Melampo Cinematografica/Cinetext Bildarchiv. Still from *To Be or Not To Be* (p. 193): © Spiegel Media GmbH. Still from Mel Brooks's *The Producers* (p. 226): © Crossbow Productions/MGM/Springtime Productions/Cinetext Bildarchiv. Photograph of a break on the set of *The Great Dictator* (p. 194): © Charlie Chaplin Productions/Cinetext Bildarchiv. Comic strip *Adolf, the Nazi Sow* by Walter Moers (p. 228): Taken from *Adolf. Äch bin wieder da!!* by Walter Moers © Eichborn AG, July 1988. Photograph and documents of pastor J. Müller (p. 200–202): © Bistumsarchiv Hildesheim. Judgment of Marianne Elise Kürschner (p. 198–199): Courtesy of Bundesarchiv, signatory: NJ 3670 (AZ: 10 J 405 / 43g). Photograph of Fritz Petter with his chimpanzee (p. 108), 1933 program for Erika Mann's *Pfeffermühle* (p. 114): Taken from *Satire gegen Hitler—Kabarett im Exil* by Reinhard Hippen. Pendo Verlag, Zürich 1986. Image on p. 203: Taken from Landesarchiv NRW, Hauptstaatsarchiv Düsseldorf RW 58 Nr. 25083 BI. 17. Cartoons of Hitler as the Grim Reaper (p. 105) and Hitler as an Indian (p. 106): Reprinted from Hitler in der Karikatur der Welt by Putzi Hanfstaengel, Verlag Braune Bücher, Berlin 1933.Photograph of Kurt Gerron at age 30, 1927 (p. 116), photograph of Kurt Gerron in the Theresienstadt concentration camp, 1944 (p. 119), still from *A Song, A Kiss, A Girl* featuring Fritz Grünbaum and Oskar Sima, 1932 (p. 115), photograph of Robert Dorsay (p. 204), announcement of Dorsay's execution addressed to his wife (p. 205): Reprinted from Ulrich Liebe: *Verehrt, Verfolgt, Vergessen*, Beltz Verlag, Weinheim—Berlin, 1992. Cartoons taken from *Der Stürmer* (p. 117–118): Reprinted from *Lieber Stürmer—Leserbriefe an das NS-Kampfblatt*, Seewald Verlag, Stuttgart 1978.